This book is available for purchase on Amazon.

ISBN: 9798870511818

First Edition

When your reality is nothing like what others experience, how do you live your life like everyone else?

Driven by a manic episode, Lara finds herself far from home in unfamiliar territory and distraught by the schizoid delusions being whispered to her by her old friends. In an effort to make them leave her in peace for even a few minutes, Lara makes a snap decision that sends her on the wildest ride of her life! There she unveils the dark side of her heart and psyche. She relives some key life moments and just maybe gains some wisdom along the way.

-Chandalee Helms

I dedicate this book to my beautiful Mom and my ex-fiancé, Bobo. I'm sure my ex-fiancé seems unorthodox, but he's still one of the most important people in my life. This journey started about 16 years ago when I typed my first words to apologize to Bobo for me not showing up and fighting for our relationship. It was hard for me.

I didn't know how to love.

I originally wanted to just give it to Bobo, and my mom without publishing it, but I know, Bobo. I feel he wouldn't read it unless it gained traction through the publishing world. Now I realize it's meant to be shared with everyone.

I also want to include a surprising motivator who was about 12 years old at the time, one of my beautiful nieces whom I call "Twinkie Snickers". I included her in a conversation about all the books that I started and innocently she said, "Auntie, when are you going to finish one?" Now it's almost two decades later and I did!

Also, I want to thank one of my dearest friends, Chris Helms, for his character of being so loving, sweet and accommodating. His sister, Chandalee Helms, did a fantastic job editing. She was so patient with me and hopefully a friend for life.

And finally, I also want to thank Robert Mazak who guided me every step of the way to publishing on Amazon and making it complete.

My biography

I was born and raised in San Antonio, Texas and lived here most of my life. I always loved to tell a story through dance or literature. In high school, I continued this passion for dance and rose through the ranks to become the Colonel of our dance team. I continued this passion for dance as an exotic entertainer once I left high school. I danced at "hole in the walls" as well as many famous strip clubs in New York City. I was offered to model for Men's Magazines but didn't pursue it because a gut feeling told me not to.

I always had an affinity for writing and studied journalism for a year. Now it is my dream to finish a novel - finish anything really. I was diagnosed bipolar I (one) schizoaffective disorder when I was age 22; now I'm 44. My diagnosis kept my mind busy while I was in bed. Starting projects were easy, and not finishing them were easy too.

This book is for the wild at heart, the "not normal", and the insensitive who find it hard to love especially with a mental illness. Through this account of hateful and shameful activity maybe this book could reunite families and the curious who may not understand. Thank God my family never left.

The Devil Taught Me How To Love

Lara Lee Murphy

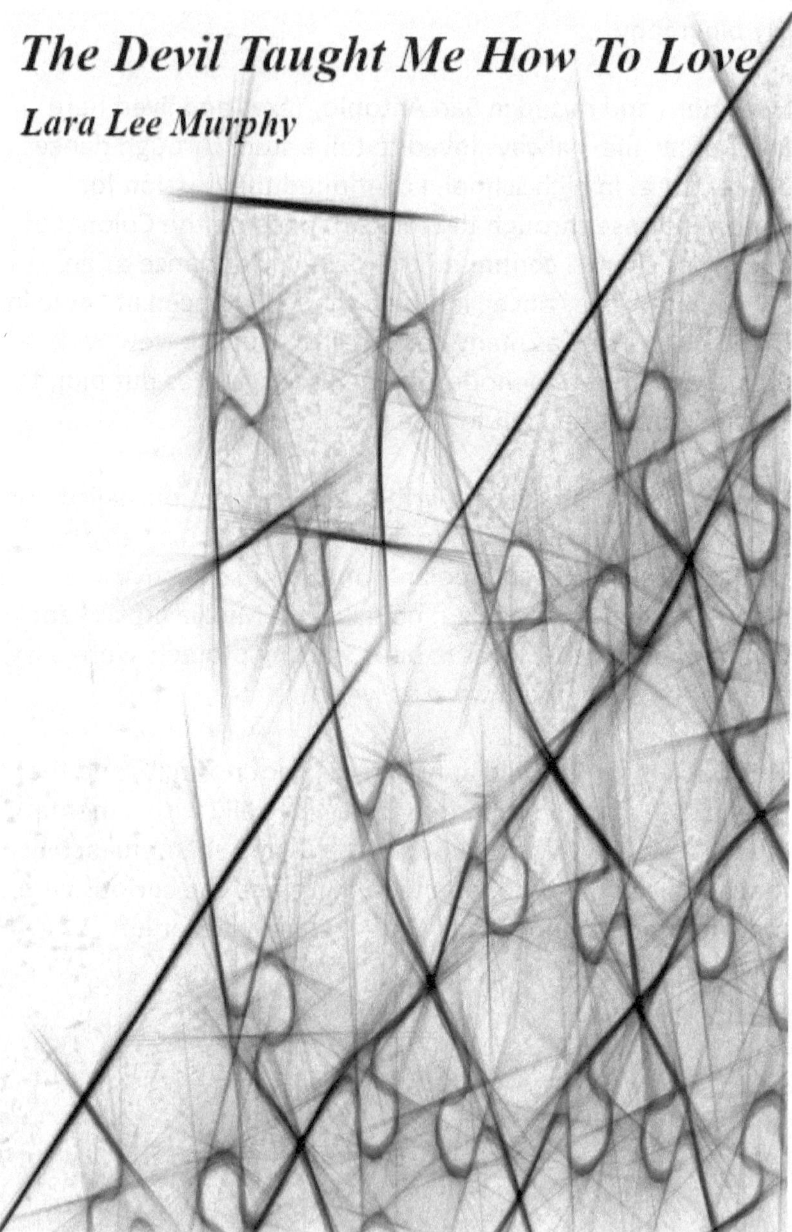

Chapter 1

The train flew around the corner while I sat on a cold concrete bench in the New Jersey subway station. In between my legs, it felt like a plunger was sucking me in and out, throbbing and pulsing in and out. In and out. The feeling had been going on for nearly 30 minutes now.

This was the most intense, and yet the worst, dirtiest and filthiest orgasm I had ever had in my life. I despised it.

It was ten years ago that the doctors diagnosed me with bipolar type 1 schizoaffective disorder. I was having a manic-psychotic episode which included grandiose thoughts, rash decisions, hallucinations, and delusions including - voices and sensations no one else could hear, imagine, or understand.

There was no one near me, no one inside me, just sadistic male voices in my head that took turns taunting me.

Upon entering the station, I was in luck because there was no attendant behind the glass making sure I'd pay. Since I had no money nor metro card, I jumped the turnstile. I took this as a sign toward following my impulse to commit suicide today.

The train was getting closer and would be arriving soon. My vagina was wet as I rushed to the platform edge and waited.

I could not. I could not jump in front of this train. I chickened out that time.

*"If you get on **this** train, you will keep the pleasure going, slut,"* the collective sadistic voice taunted.

I have battled these voices in my head for years and years. It seemed like forever that they had chimed in and told me what to think, say and do. At this point, they were also my best friends; they knew every intimate part of my brain and I felt I had no one else but them.

The unwanted orgasm made me feel like a two-cent whore, good for no one. I was too vain, and it was going to fuck with me like the vain, selfish whore I felt I was. It wouldn't stop unless I killed myself.

I was morally humiliated, and for the first time, I felt like a horrible person. I had hurt others, left my family and my fiancé, whom I affectionately called Bobo.

The subway was all shades of green, like the witch's view in the movie, *The Wizard of OZ.*

My body parts were throbbing and pulsing like the erratic heartbeat of someone on meth. Thump... Thump - thump... Thump - thump... Thump - thump... Thump - thump. Sometimes the orgasm got a whimper out of me, my back arched, my head rose, otherwise, I held it together. But then, I wouldn't allow the voices to have control over me anymore.

The voices threatened that the orgasms would keep going if I stepped inside this **first** train. Because of this, I backed away from the edge. I would jump in front when the next one pushed through. No way did I want to keep *"this 'pleasure' going!"* as they threatened.

Still, I would not leave the path toward death today. I would take control and die today!

Part of my condition, schizoaffective disorder, is like schizophrenia, but different because the diagnosis also includes an emotional disorder like bipolar. My schizoaffective hallucinations were audible, visible, tangible and I could smell and taste what other people called an illusion.

If I had input from at least one of my five senses, what I perceived was real. I was the only one aware of them as far as I knew. These so-called hallucinations were the real truth, the real world, the creativity behind the scenes of everyone else's boring life.

Bipolar I (one) disorder includes severe confusion of "reality", rapid speech, flying from one subject to the next, hypersexuality, skyrocket energy, grandiose ideas, and no need to rest or sleep.

In my case, depending on the episode and the day, I wholeheartedly believed I was either God, the Devil, Joan of Arc or even Marilyn Monroe. I always pushed my friends and family away from me. I hated them. My hatred for them grew because I couldn't act like myself. No one understood me.

My only desire was for my family and friends to not judge me, let me be free. My family and friends were my enemies because if I did act unusual, they would lock me up in a mental hospital that could take a month for release.

It would seem most of society's enemies were my friends. For example, rapists, an enemy to most people, were still my friends. It was like, I would rather a rapist take my body but not my inner sanctum by being locked in an asylum. In the hospitals I would be drugged to behave like 99 percent of the normal people in the United States today. The rapist may become a murderer, but my mind would still be free.

Normal people were always the ones who'd ask that philosophical question, "What's normal?" Then they would puff up their chest and look at me like they just said something so profound, and it made them chuckle. To these people I said, having an orgasm from spirits while waiting for any train to jump in front of and commit suicide is "not normal."

A black vortex was spiraling through my chest. It was an empty cold feeling in the center of me. I could see it and feel it. I was empty as if my heart had disintegrated into nothing. I had left my family and completely accepted I'd never see them again. I left my home, and I left my fiancé Bobo who I've been with off and on for seven years - the best man in the world. I left them all to find Donny, my ex-boyfriend who had been an ex since 2001. Here I was ten years later.

My hometown was San Antonio, Texas. I flew to the northeast coast to see my ex-boyfriend, Donny, even if just one more time.

I could hear subliminal messages through the radio cloud in slow distortion before purchasing my plane tickets from Texas. The whispers along the radio waves were saying if I made it to New York City, the voices would reunite me with Donny. I had not seen or heard from him in almost a decade. He did not know I was coming; it was my surprise to him. When I bought my plane ticket, I didn't realize the destination was to New Jersey, not New York City; I was manic and confused.

The voices lied to me; Donny never showed up when I waited for him those cold September nights on the streets of Jersey. So currently, here I was in a subway station.

My name is Lara. My shirt had small, needle sized holes through it and was stained with ink from my writer's pen. My army pants didn't zip up and I was wearing loose combat boots. For weeks I hadn't eaten, and I rarely slept. I was too busy plotting how I was going to change the world.

My mousy brown hair looked like it was cut with a child's safety scissors. It was just uneven stubble from my scalp. Because of that most strangers thought I was gay, and even asked if I was. Judgmental bastards.

People also called me druggie because I was boney and hyper, talking as fast as my mind was racing. When manic, nearly everyone thought I was on a drug. The real high I got, however, was the chemical imbalance in the brain. Bipolar disorder was a mental haywire; it was a natural drug.

When this manic episode started, I was taking my meds, but the days rapidly passed, and I forgot that I even had meds to take.

I went back and dropped on the cold hard bench in the tunnel. The crowd of a dozen or so had no clue what was going on inside me. My vagina pulsing from orgasms caused by unseen spirits and me trying to plan my death.

"I know you like this. Tighten your legs as much as you can, it won't stop Bitch. You love yourself too much to kill yourself. Too vain," the voices' ultra-consciousness continued.

I didn't hate the voices, but then again, I wasn't normal. The voices were sometimes my friends when they made me feel special. At other times, they damned and demeaned me.

I was sore, swollen, and ashamed by the moisture in between my legs. As if my legs weren't already clinched shut, my hands gripped like bolts of steel onto the concrete bench, sealing my legs together further.

"Now! Now!" I thought with anticipation. Here it approaches, the **second** train. It was going slow, slower than I had hoped. I was certain; I was going to jump anyway. The voices were convinced that I wasn't going to do it. I fought their dominance over me, their idea of me, like a stubborn child. I violently nodded, "I WILL jump, I will, I am, watch me!" I declared.

It felt like I was about to throw myself away. Who cares? It was easy. It was easy to throw myself away when I never felt like I existed anyway. Here came the train. Just a hop, skip, jump, and vanish, as easy as that. The humiliation inside me would end, I felt dead anyway, and this was Hell. "Ready and go," I told myself. Then the voices rapidly, and desperately chimed in, *"We'll leave you alive but disabled!"*

I paused. Alive but physically disabled?

I didn't want to be alive and physically disabled! In my mind, my voices made an image of me being stuck in a wheelchair without any limbs to even roll the wheels.

The sign on the front of this second train read the destination was, "Road to Hell".

"Alive but disabled" was what echoed in my head leading me to forgo the plan. I stepped inside this train instead of jumping to my death. The voices didn't say the orgasms would keep going if I stepped inside this **second** train. The moment I stepped inside, the orgasms stopped. My dread turned to a calm excitement, an overdue relief. I wanted to know what was coming.

Outside the train platform was filling up with people. The people were taking out their phones, taking pictures. Some were screaming. The reason for their panic was unbeknown by me. Cops rushed to the terminal. I idly noticed all these people never got on the train I was on; they were all outside the train. I looked inside this train. Only the conductor and I were in it. Hurry! Let's go! I don't want the cops to spoil this adventure to Hell, I thought. I looked forward to the ride with anticipation.

The conductor had long, gray-silver dreads with some brown woven into it. He never looked at me. He had black, faded tats beneath his skin and he wore an orange prison jumpsuit. He was as real as I was. I could run up and feel his leathered skin if I dared. However, he looked like he didn't want to be touched. His aura was that of a God. A Rock God.

It was as if my lower limbs were spreading roots inside the train. I belonged there.

"Welcome to the crazy train, ticket for one? Then the loudspeaker overhead seemed to laugh as it jammed the song *Crazy Train* by Ozzy Osbourne.

The conductor sped off and we left the spectacle that was outside.

Chapter 2

The lights in the train flickered. The surface of the subway car plexiglass showed my complexion as even more fair, a translucent shell like a ghost. I was in rags, and I was skin and bones.

All the lights in the train shut off, car after car.

Cold air swept through the train.

From nowhere stage lights blazed outside on the terminal floor.

A velvet curtain draped along the dirty subway platform on the other side. It opened like a play was about to start. Here I watched scenes of my past appear one after another.

The curtain stayed open and the first day of acting class materialized along the subway platform.

The acting class was taught by Steven Matson at The Playhouse Studio in New York City. That was where I met Donny.

In the train, time stopped. I watched, mesmerized by the scene before me.

Donny strolled in late, seesawing the loose wood floorboard, again and again until the class laughed. Everything he did was funny to them. I didn't laugh. What was funny?

Throughout the day, everything he did made the class giggle or roar with laughter. I didn't get it.

Donny and I were paired for the first assignment to perform a play in front of the class. It was about a lover's quarrel where the male actor was using his girlfriend for money and sex. In the play, the female character fell in love too quickly.

Donny and I waited to practice the scenes together until the night before the presentation. We agreed to meet at his place.

The subway ride from my apartment in Washington Heights that was North of Harlem, to Donny's flat didn't seem too long, maybe 30 minutes. He lived in the trendy, expensive apartments in Greenwich Village, Manhattan.

Donny answered his door. A musky scent of incense and burning candles wafted out to greet my senses. I walked in. He was playing a bluesy Van Morrison album. What was Donny's intention with all this ambiance?

To start, we both were relaxed. As I looked around my eyes softened as they landed on a painting, he had obviously done it himself. "That painting is beautiful," I commented. I learned later it was a painting of his first love from France.

"I taught myself how to paint," he replied.

"You're much different in person," he said. I knew exactly what he was talking about. I had made up a persona that was not the real me once I moved to "the city" to protect myself. I found that was what was needed to be respected in the city. So, I acted like a different person even in acting class. No one knew I wasn't a real bitch. I was just good at this roleplaying. It was fun to trick even the acting coaches.

It was amusing that they had no clue I was acting all the time I was around them. They never caught on.

My walls caved in almost immediately for Donny though. To him I was soft, he even said my aura was a light pink color. "Let's pull an all-nighter," he said eagerly. I desired to go home and sleep for at least a few hours before our 10 a.m. class. But Donny had a vision in his mind of how he wanted the play to be directed. He watched too many Marlon Brando films in my opinion. He was focused, manic even. We put this rehearsal off way too long for us to remember everything for showtime. Block left, now move forward, then get in my face and yell. That part was fun for me. It went on all night.

The next day was showtime in front of the class. My acting sucked, my sense of direction was off, and all my lines left me cold. The play was a disaster. There were bags under my eyes and my face wore the disappointment in myself. Donny whispered my lines to me and motioned his head on where to go. The acting coach, Steven, didn't let it go much further.

After class, Donny and I went over to an Irish bar. We slammed several shots of tequila on the table and then chugged it down.

The more drunk we got, the more we got to know each other. The alcohol weakened my carefully constructed walls of protection. Maybe it did the same for him.

"Are you from here?" I asked.

"No, I'm from Kenya, Africa," he said without a specific accent.

"What made you come to the U.S.?" I inquired.

"I followed my girlfriend on a student visa to NYU. I chose acting here after we broke up.

"Why acting?" I asked.

"I'm curious about human behavior," he answered.

"You?" he prompted.

"I want to live in other's shoes and find our common traits. Basically, I want to live more fully," I explained.

"So, you're from Texas you said earlier; what brings you to New York by yourself?" he inquired of me.

"Well, unlike you following your girlfriend to New York, I ran as far away as I could from an ex," I replied. "We were on and off for five years. It was a very dysfunctional relationship. So yeah, I sold all my furniture and saved $10,000 to get here. I came here with lots of hopes, big dreams, and only one bag of clothes."

"Whoa, $10,000! Was that without help from your family?" He kept the flow of conversation going. I wasn't used to that with men. Usually, men just want to have sex with me, not to know who I was.

"Yep," I answered and explained that I had been a stripper for four years, and I still was.

He shyly confided in me that his parents were a wealthy Jewish family in Africa and were paying his bills.

An hour had passed before he said, "Let's end this sexual tension". I didn't realize there was any sexual tension. Now that he brought it up, maybe I was developing a crush on him. We started kissing, which started the path toward one thing. Oh no! Was I going to sleep with him on the first date? Was this a date? In the taxi, we kissed the entire way to his flat.

The kissing didn't end until Donny said, "I don't just want to have a one-night stand. We are both drunk, so let's not start it this way." This was new to me: consideration.

We woke up in the morning. Then we "slept together".

It was such a beautiful morning. All the window blinds were pulled up and the sun was shining brilliantly. I stretched, while Donny lit a cigarette and wrapped a sarong around himself and talked Swahili to his friend on the phone. He was sexy! He had fair skin with no tattoos, and he spoke three languages. He knew Swahili, French, and English. I was 22-years-old and he was three years older than me. We were both Aquarians.

That night, before going to a party, Donny told me he majored in psychology and philosophy at NYU. As I sat on his bed, he read me some of his dissertation papers. I looked at him blankly and he threw his papers in the trash mentioning his professor liked it anyway, and that he received a letter grade of an A.

Later that same night, Donny took me to a party with *thinkers* he went to school with. We were taking this fast. I never knew a guy to take me to meet his friends so quickly! I was happy he wanted to include me.

I didn't like crowds and I never had anything to say at a party or anywhere. But I wanted Donny beside me. Regardless, Donny went into the other room and gathered with a *selected* group of *like minds*. He left me alone in the living room; he wanted me to socialize. If Donny truly learned anything in his psychology books while at NYU, he would have known that I was an introvert and usually only comfortable with maybe one or two people - not a group of people pontificating.

I sat slumped on the couch for about an hour. I stared vacantly at the bodies in the room. I tried to plaster a smile on my mouth while I hoped no one would come and talk to me. Donny finally came over and we left.

For the rest of the days of courtship, Donny and I played like two puppies rolling around in the bed; it was nothing but bliss and fun. The start of something great!

He told me he dreamt in color and that he also had vivid daydreams. He asked if I dreamt in color, slowly and shyly I answered, "No. I wish I did".

Then, we watched a young Marlon Brando star in *The Godfather.* Donny thought he looked like Marlon Brando. He didn't, but it made me laugh. Donny had more of a James Dean vibe to him. He had swag. He was six-feet tall, had brown, wavy, short hair, and his body was slender, with muscle definition like a lean athlete.

After the movie finished, I drifted off in his arms. Before sleep, Donny turned on music with slow and melodic rhythm. I was in the kind of trance that I never wanted to wake up from. In my dream, I saw circles of different sizes swirling around my head. They were in vivid colors of royal purple, gold, and deep blue. I wasn't on any drug. I had never tried any drug at that point. Lucidly, I recognized this was a dream in color! Donny had given that to me. What a gift!

With the feeling of euphoria from the music and dreams, I could hear him hypnotizing me. "Let's never lose touch," he said. Then Donny stuck a tracking device in my arm. In my mind's eye I could see him smile and lay his head back down, while I was still off dreaming.

I didn't mind if he wanted us to stay together forever even if we temporally lose touch; that's what this device meant to me.

The next day I spent at Donny's' house, I was looking for a pen. I opened a drawer, and it had a dozen or so medications in it. I didn't want to bring it up; it was none of my business. Sure enough, that morning, he said he was bipolar, and he decided to stop taking his meds. "So, that's what all those pills were for!" I exclaimed.

Donny's eyes got wide, and he looked at me, pissed. He thought I was rummaging through his things, being nosey. "I was searching for a pen," I said. "I thought you'd bring it up when you were ready," I continued. He looked happy again like he saw a piece of me that's rare - someone who didn't judge him.

Donny explained pieces of what it was like to be bipolar. He admitted he was severely stressed after the relationship with his first love ended. He had his first episode, and the hospital wouldn't let him out for over a month.

"They keep you locked up!" he said. He looked into my eyes, "You have big pupils!" he said. "They're dilated!" he exclaimed.

So? I thought.

"So do you!" I exclaimed back. Then he began asking me questions.

"Do you ever feel like people are following you, or that people talk directly to you through the television?"

I knew he was trying to see if I was bipolar too, but the conversation was cut short when his mom called to remind him to renew his visa before it expired.

Donny soon backed off after the short courtship. We switched. He became aloof, but I had found and kept his missing heart. I worked, and worked, and worked at a strip club when we weren't spending time together to keep my mind occupied. I had been a stripper since I was 18 years old. It was four years in the making.

The few days I stayed with Donny, the more attached I became. I started becoming a needy, clingy woman and all my insecurities transferred into desperation. I showed up at his flat unannounced all the time; I hated who I had become. "Don't break my heart, Donny. Please, don't break my heart. I couldn't survive," was the mantra that came from my soul.

Chapter 3

Two months down the road, in the middle of the night, Donny knocked on my door loudly a few times to wake me up. I threw on cutoff jean shorts and a pink vintage top. He asked if I wanted to go to our mutual friends, Lanna and Stash's house. I was so excited to hang out with friends, and him, even if it was 3 a.m. and without notice.

Once there, Lanna asked me to change into something sexier. She grabbed a short, white, cotton slip that fit perfectly. "Do you want to try ecstasy, Lara?" Lanna asked.

"Yeah!" I exclaimed. I wanted to experience it for the first time, particularly with Donny.
I witnessed myself in a mirror. My eyes grew wide, and my huge pupils took over the blue part of my irises. It looked like an eclipse moon shadowing the sun.
Donny started kissing me. Stash and Lanna stared from the couch as Donny began to lift up the slip exposing my upper thighs all the way to my breasts. I pulled it back down.
Donny smirked and said, "Okay". It was about 5 a.m. when we left. Donny went to his apartment solo, and I guessed I had to go back to my apartment alone also. No one had sex, thank God.
Donny and I dated for six months. Really, I dated him. My heart was in it, he just wanted me to keep him company, I guess. Really, he just wanted the badge of dating a stripper. That's what our friend Lanna was always trying to tell me.

In the sixth month, I was going to Donny's studio apartment to collect $1,000 that I loaned him for a high-tech spy camera.

Donny liked to capture human behavior on film for some reason without them knowing. I kept pushing hard for him to pay me back for months until he finally had the money to do it.

He leaned over to one side of his desk, and he paid me; Donny looked disgusted at me, while calling me the most hurtful names. He said I was pathetic, and under his thumb, and more. I left his apartment feeling worse than I ever felt at that point.

I could not fight the tears away on the subway ride home. A horrible stabbing pain afflicted me, cutting my gut like a long-jagged knife. It was cold, painful, and left me hollow. This could not be real. My pain turned into insecurity. It was apparent he was seeing someone else.

Was she pretty? I wondered. Donny got me to stop wearing makeup. He wanted me to look natural, and humble looking with my mousy brown hair and no more Doc Marten's, nor heels, just regular tennis shoes. That apparently didn't help him love me.

Creepily, when he wasn't home, I went to his apartment once and sniffed his cologne under the door.

I went to Starbucks by the subway exit to his abode, and I sat there for hours to see if he'd come by because he wasn't answering my calls. Trying not to seem desperate, I only called him obsessively every day, and every day he didn't answer. The more he ignored me the more I begged.

I was pathetic like he said, and ugly in my mind. I was uncontrollable.

A week later, Donny wanted me to come over. I went. For the first time, Donny and I made love. It was quick. During, he said he did love me for the first time and asked me to marry him. Amid everything, he handed me a rose quartz and told me it can heal my heart and that I would always remember him by it. I didn't say anything, I just kissed him like it was the last time. I left his apartment after that.

I was leaving the next day to spend a few weeks with my family in San Antonio, Texas. The trip was preplanned before all this drama. I thought I would come back, and Donny and I could pick up where we left off.

The night before my departure, my friend Lanna took me to a bar and as I cried, she explained everything. Donny asked another woman to marry him, and they were getting married in a month in France! Hastily, I wanted to bang on Donny's door, even break it down, but I knew he wouldn't be home anyway; he was seeing someone else. I knew that, but the truth in our friend Lanna's eyes and concern for me was the confirmation needed.

This all felt like a bad dream. It was as if I could wake up and everything would be better. It would not be better.

The curtain closed.

Coming back to the train ride, the conductor paused the train, and I could still see Donny's face lingering until we rolled past him.

Chapter 4

Through the windowpane of the train, I could see the image of myself in my childhood bedroom pacing without rest while I visited my mom and family in San Antonio, Texas.

The curtain reopened.

"I'm manic, I'm manic, I'm bipolar, I know I am bipolar," I chanted like Native Americans did for rain, listening to a Disturbed song, *Down with the Sickness.*
I wanted to be bipolar, to be as smart as Donny. I wanted to have knowledge, not bliss. I had been blissful my whole life and I felt I was taken advantage of. Everyone called me sweetie. And by that point, I hated it! I felt no one took me seriously. Now they would see what I was made of. I have special powers. That night I called Donny about a dozen times. He never answered. I left several messages and yelled through the machine that I was going to change the world! My mom woke up happy to see me at the breakfast table. After all, it had been about a year since I had seen her. My mom wanted to chat. I didn't sleep all night. She wanted my smile and attention for her. She wanted a glimpse that I was still somewhere in my hollow eyes. She wanted to see that I still loved her and life itself like I used to.
I tried to ignore her. She didn't ignore me. I gave short answers. She kept questioning. "Sweetie," she said, "What's wrong? It looks like you've been crying." I did not tell her about Donny.

"Please don't call me sweetie any more Mom. I'm tired of being known as sweetie. I have stuff to do," I said matter-of-factly.
"Did you get some sleep?" she asked.
"No." I said curtly. She didn't know what to say.
The curtain outside the train closed.

Chapter 5

The curtain reopened.

The lights on the subway platform lit up, and out came the next scene of my past as I viewed from inside the train. Shortly after I came back to San Antonio, I visited my first ex-boyfriend from years ago, Chaz. Chaz was the one I flew to New York City to avoid. His sister told him I was in town, and he invited me to a party.
I was so happy to get invited to a party from him; I thought of him as a long-lost friend, nothing more. I was eager to go to get my mind off things. Once there, Chaz and I played chess! Wow! Chess! I loved it. I barely had this time with Donny and never with Chaz. Before, I was a sex object to both of them.
Chaz gave me a pill. He said, "Here take this; it's a muscle relaxer." I took it. I exclaimed to the whole party, "This isn't a muscle relaxer, this is ecstasy!"
"Be quiet!" Chaz hissed.
I wanted to keep playing chess, but Chaz took me by the hand to his bedroom and fucked me. Afterwards he kicked me out by saying he had something to do in the morning. I only slept with Chaz because for some reason I felt he expected it. Besides, the ecstasy also hindered my wishes to stay true to Donny. I wasn't strong enough to say no. Nothing was ever special between Chaz and me.

After Chaz kicked me out, I felt the heat of anger like an erupting volcano inside of me. Chaz's sister was a friend of mine. She knew I was under the influence of ecstasy, so she offered to take me to my mom's. I got inside her car but opened the door and jumped out while the car was moving. "No, Lara!" she exclaimed.

I jumped out anyway and banged on Chaz's door amid his party. No one opened the door, but I heard laughter, so I called him. One woman answered the phone and the only thing she said was "Rock", and then hung up.

That's a clue! I thought. Rock music will be on my radio dial for the rest of my life! I'll listen for the subliminal signs and follow the maze towards Donny from now on. Donny was my prize in the mix. The maze was any sign including my throbbing arm from the tracking device that Donny put there when we were first together. Yep, I thought, it would mean he was thinking about me. I must find him until the pieces fit.

Regardless of Chaz's sister wanting to give me a ride home, since I drove my silver Firebird to the party, I'd drive it back home. It was sweet of her, but I had my own ride. I left my Firebird at my mom's when I moved to NYC. I always rode the subways when I was in New York.

I now expected the radio would speak to me. It was a secret and I never told anyone that this woman said "Rock". Why would anyone in their right mind just answer the phone, say that, and then hang up? I was beginning to look crazy to others but found a direction towards the unknown. No one would ever have a clue as to what I was talking about. I didn't care. The GPS device Donny put in my arm was pulsing.

The curtain shut.

Chapter 6

The conductor sped up and I had to hold onto a pole.

My forearm was throbbing from the tracking device Donny put inside of my arm, back when he hypnotized me. What did Donny want me to do? I could only guess.

"Let's never lose touch," those were the words he said that never left my mind. He's tricking me again. He's not really going to marry another woman! He put this object inside me for some reason. Donny must be thinking of me. I swore inside the train.

As quickly as the scene closed from the episode with Chaz, out came the next scene with my mom again, all still in San Antonio.

The curtain reopened.

All night in my childhood room my radio was on the rock station. While I dozed off for an hour or so, I'd wake up when the bands Korn, Disturbed, or Tool took over the airwaves. These bands I resonated with. Daylight came and I still felt the effects of the ecstasy Chaz gave me.

To get ready for work usually took hours; this time, I did not want to take a shower, shave, nor wash my hair, so I didn't. I was in the mood to go, go, go! I put on minimal makeup and stuffed my bag with costumes and left with greasy hair.

My mom saw me leave the house with my duffle bag. A look of disapproval swept through her eyes. Regardless she said, "Have a good day sweetie". I was out the door to work the dayshift into the night. It would be a thirteen-hour workday. My mind must get off Donny.

I stopped at the local gas station to fuel up. Two strange men stared at me. Finally, one of them asked if I could give them a ride to somewhere up North. Believing what they said about their car not working, I said "Okay". It would be another adventure I thought, no more questions asked.

To experience mania, it was as if the wind had a color to it, like the painting Starry Night from Van Gogh, but in real life. Nothing made sense, everything was sporadic and euphoric. We were on the road now for nearly an hour and my nerves were on edge. There was a rest stop and the men got out of the car gleefully to stretch their legs and pee. Before exiting my sports car, they mentioned carving their names on the picnic tables. I was offended. Just because they rode with the famous Lara Lee, they wanted others to know I took them there. Their scribble will remain there as a part of history, a famous story about me. I was sure.

Another hour passed and it was time to let this joy ride end. "At the next pit stop, y'all need to find another ride," I said assertively. They adamantly refused and said they didn't know of anyone who could pick them up so far away. One of them got on his cell phone and said he found them a ride. At the next rest stop, they got out of the car, but not before stealing all the quarters that were in my cup holders. It was amazing to me how many people only care about money. I just rolled my eyes and took off. In my state of mind, it felt like I was taken advantage of by many people, for example, Chaz and these fools.

I tended to my day. I rode back to work at Shh! Strip club.

Chapter 7

Once inside the club, I was hungry, I had not eaten for days. I went to the kitchen to order a salad. The cook, Zack, who always flirted with me said he was getting off work soon. He said he'd make the salad before he left for the night. He asked afterwards if I wanted to get in his truck to go have some fun. Fun sounded like my main objective, so I said, "Ok!"

We headed West and were on the road for about an hour. I fell asleep. Zack began touching my boobs. I woke up to the sound of trucks roaring their engines. The men in the different trucks were following us to make sure I was safe. They were without question my rock star friends. Apparently, they saw what Zack was doing to me. They disapproved and wanted me to jump out of Zack's truck. On the highway, I opened the truck door to jump out. We were going about 60 or 70 miles per hour. "No!" Zack screamed, then pulled off onto the access road. That's when I jumped out. I had no socks or shoes on. I took them off in the truck to be comfortable. They were left on the floorboard when I was so hasty to get out. Zack got out of the truck too and tried to grab me around the waist to hoist me back in. Passersby saw what was happening. Zack got back into his vehicle and sped off out of sight.

I was not worried nor even cared about him at this moment. It was getting late, and dusk was setting in. I ran across the highway and then walked across the last lane because I had no fear of death. I was invincible. Immediately a car screeched to a stop on the active highway, inches from my heels and blasted his horn. I flipped him off. I was so close to death but didn't give a fuck.

Turned out I jumped out of Zack's vehicle at the right time because after I ran across the highway there was a massive movie theatre. It was as if put there by God for me to find. I walked confidently without socks or shoes, but I had my keys in my pocket the whole time. I was wearing a green hoodie, midriff top, and tight jeans. *Passion of the Christ* was playing that night. I asked a man with his wife if he could pay for the ticket to get me in. After he noticed my bare feet, he gave me the money! His wife looked at me, then at him, her mouth was open, and her eyes wide in shock.

During the movie, I put my feet on top of the vacant seat in front of me. I didn't watch any part with Jesus in it. My head stayed down. Somehow the Devil caught my attention when she appeared on the screen. Then, and only then, did I watch the cinema. It was not like I have seen this before, so how did I know when the Devil would show her face? She looked like me with my hoodie on.

After the show, people who passed by noticed me. One way or another, I caught people's attention.

I walked out of the movie theatre without a ride. It was dark outside, night.

I knew I'd be okay. At play and for no reason, I moved my legs and arms in the grass making grass angels similar to snow angels but with grass. Onlookers passed by slowly as if they were witnessing something rare or a bad car accident. One man stopped his car and asked if I needed a ride.

"Why yes," I said. This stranger reached over and opened the passenger side door for me. He looked to be around 23 years old, the same age as me. His car was a simple four door Toyota and blue; it was clean inside. "I need to go to Shh! strip club," I affirmed.

"Okay, I have to get something first," he said and then drove us to his house.

He went inside his house, and I turned his radio dial to the rock station while waiting inside his car.

He returned with a pair of men's white socks.

"Here, these are to keep your feet warm," he said.

It was summer, but I loved men's socks. They always made me feel cozy and safe. He must have known.

After about the tenth loop through this guy's neighborhood, I asked, "What are you doing? Where are we going? You are supposed to take me to my car at Shh!"

"I showcased you to the neighborhood to let my neighbors know I got you," he said.

"Oh, ok," I said. He drove me around because I was famous through my new rock star friends. I remembered the woman at Chaz's party that only said, "Rock", and hung up. So, yes, all these people on the radio knew who I was and were my new friends. So, I understood why he paraded me to his neighborhood.

In the subway train, as I watched this scene from the past unfold, I remembered telling my therapist after this episode at the mental hospital how everyone knew who I was. She said it was all a delusion in my head, a sign of mania. I remember saying, "Well, why did he want to present me to his friends?"

The therapist then said, "He was playing the game. He knew you were insane and wanted to use you, so he played up what was in your imagination."

After carting me around, this guy - I didn't know his name - was just another stranger who took me far away in his car. We ended up at a huge park that was alive with people. It was around 10 p.m. and all these people were still out. I was uncomfortable and what made it worse was when we got out of the car and sat on the grass, this guy started massaging me. The tips of his fingers spread a chill to my soul. I was scared.

Noticing all these people in the park, I believed they were here to see me because I was a friend of rock stars, or so I thought. Standing up I broke the spell this guy was trying to achieve with his massage, and I walked up to several cars full of people. I knocked on each of their windows and when they rolled it down, I said, "I know what you're doing". I did this to about five different cars. Each of them left after I told them that. I just wanted them to know that I knew they were just here to see me, that's it; that was all I wanted to tell them.

The guy who brought me here said, "Did you notice when you go up to these cars they leave?"

"They are embarrassed," I said. "I caught them in the act of spying on me."

He continued to rub his spiney hands on me. "I want to go back," I demanded.

"In a minute," he said.

"No, you're scaring me!" I raised my voice. "I want to get my car!"

This unnamed man took me back in town to Shh! strip club. Once there, I noticed my car had been stolen.

The club was closed.

I banged on the doors to the club and kept protesting for them to let me in. Finally, after a few minutes Chuck, the night manager, opened the door. I saw what looked to be basketball players vacuuming the floor. There was nothing fake in my imagination, so I knew these over 9-feet tall good-looking guys were real. They just stared at me.

"My car was stolen!" I told Chuck.

"I think it got repossessed my dear," Chuck said and reached out his hand for me to come in.

I forgot to continue making my payments while I was in NYC. Regardless, I could not believe it was repossessed. It was stolen; I was sure.

I hysterically denied what Chuck said about my car even though he insisted and took me to my mom's. He gave me his digits and said if I ever needed a ride, let him know. Working was the only thing that got my mind off Donny. I was super skinny from being a vegan and not eating because I wasn't hungry. I was also never hungry when depressed. So, it was understandable that people at the club would think I was on drugs.

Chuck gave me a ride the following night to the club. I was
gaunt, wired, had mood fluctuations, paranoid, and wearing
one fishnet stocking on one leg and not the other. I thought
I would make what I was wearing a fashion statement that
others would follow.
At work, I got on stage and screamed, "What am I seeing?" I
faked that one. I saw nothing. I don't know why I said that.
Managers rushed me off the stage, and I said, "No, no, I'm
better now. I don't see anything". They took me to the
changing room where I had plenty of drinks in me.
One of the dancers said, "Oh no, here comes that druggie,
again." I did two drugs in my life besides drinking. I was
offended. I exclaimed back, "I am a messenger from God! I
am Joan of Arc!"
They had no heart, they were cruel. I WASN'T ON DRUGS!
That ecstasy was a few nights ago.
The manager, Chuck, had me wait in his office. The strippers
were cackling at me. The dancers' gossip and laughter
roared till each entertainer got their goods and left. They
just couldn't accept I was a messenger from God. Chuck
drove me home to my mom's house about 40 miles away.
He was so nice. Chuck told me to call if I needed a ride at all,
tomorrow, or whenever.
The curtain closed.

Chapter 8

The curtain opened.

In the next scene, it seemed Chuck was taking me for a joy
ride in his Mercedes.
We were on the back roads to Shh!, the club we worked at.
Chuck asked me what radio station I liked. He put it on a
rock station as suggested. I took off my boots and rested my
feet on the dash of his Mercedes.
He opened his sunroof and just for fun I stood on the seat
and let my hair blow in the wind. I poured the water that
was in my water bottle all over the window. I was a girl just
having fun. Chuck screamed, "I just washed my car!" Who
cares? I thought. Play.
I was headbanging to loud rock music. People in other
vehicles stared, not like staring at a car wreck, but just like
they never saw someone have so much fun. I'm sure it was
weird to their mundane lives.
Eventually, I sat back down when we got close to the club. A
song by Chevelle came on the radio, called "The Red". At
that point I decided, I would lay down. I opened the car door
and proceeded to jump out. Chuck forcefully screamed,
grabbed my arm, and called out my stage name, "Angel"!
"Get back in! Get in!" Chuck then slowed down realizing I
was mad and not listening. I was able to scrape my feet on
the ground and jump out.
I laid in the middle of the road with a car coming close, but it
swerved around me.

The people in the car swerved, looked in disbelief and one got her phone. They're calling to spread the word. They're spreading the word to the world I'm Jesus reincarnate now. Chuck left me in the middle of the road, jetting out of the scene in his silver Mercedes.

Before I left the house that morning, my mom, a nurse, said she thought I was bipolar and going manic. She read about it. The trigger was when I told her I was Jesus, and I wasn't sleeping. She said I had all the signs, for instance believing I was a rock star, a muse, or even God.

Barefoot, I took to the street. The cement was hot, but Jesus walked on water, so I could afford walking on this sun-beaten pavement, gathering blisters as I walked along.

Like a child at play, I picked up what I could find, sticks. There was no reason for this at all, just playing.

That's when the police stopped it all and took me somewhere else.

The curtain closed.

Chapter 9

The curtain reopened.

The stage on the train platform turned to white walls and I could feel draped over me the hospital's chilly, sickly, unwashed blankets even through the plexiglass of the subway.
The cops took me to the hospital. I thought they took me there because I was a genius about to be evaluated.
The bug-eyed nurses in scrubs seemed to size me up for their giant think tank behind their observation plexiglass, evaluating my every move.
On my first day there at the governmental hospital, an employee, about my age of 22, carried on a conversation with me. He dressed as if he was in a band. I found out later he was. He had tats and huge earring holes and skater sneakers. We talked a lot about nothing. He asked if I had a boyfriend and I said "Yes, Donny."
I imagined to myself Donny was still my boyfriend even though he was probably already married to that girl as we stood there talking. I wrapped a rubber band around my ring finger to remember he asked me to marry him that moment we made love. It was our last encounter.

During dinner at the hospital, I was sure I was drugged with ecstasy because I knew the feeling of the narcotic. The other reason I thought the employees drugged me was because they set my tray aside, had guilty faces and my intuition simply knew. After eating dinner, I felt awake and alert. My pupils were also dilated. I was happy and wanted to stay up all night.

After dinner, I told John (he's the employee that befriended me) about my fear of being drugged. He agreed and said that he could tell by my eyes and how I was acting.

My feet dangled off a short brick ledge inside the hospital as John and I talked. He said, "I want to show you something". He took me into the storage unit and tried to kiss me! I said, pushing him back, "Whoa! I have a boyfriend".

He said, "I thought you were kidding." He was upset with me. Really, really unglued.

He told me I had to go to bed early. I did. I never told on him. He was my friend. I wondered if that was the reason the employees drugged me. John wanted to take advantage of me.

I was in bed, restless. Then I experienced the worst constipation ever. I tried to handle it, sleep even, but there was no stopping the pain. After midnight, I walked up to the nurse at the help desk and asked for a laxative. She was so cruel to me!

"You should have asked me before you went to bed," she scolded.

I went to the restroom and tried to push it out myself to no avail. I then went back to the nurse.

"Please, it hurts!" I hunched over and grabbed my belly.
"I've tried pushing it out in the bathroom several times. I can't do it on my own!"
"Tough shit!" she said.
"No-shit!" I answered.
"Try putting your fingers up there and dig it out," the nurse concluded.
I took her gross advice and relieved the pain.
A few days later, I waited in a line that circled around the corner for meds. I crashed down to my knees and dug my fingers into my skull. This was my first panic attack. The pain was inside my innermost muscles, and I couldn't itch it. No one would understand.
A nurse came by and asked if I was okay, but I didn't know how to describe what was happening to me.
Finally, up at the medication desk, the panic attack subsided. The nurse gave me my pills that I didn't swallow. "Stick out your tongue," she said to check if I took them. "Ok, you're staying longer," she said after she saw the evidence of pills in my mouth.
After about a month, I found out I wasn't getting out of this institution. During recess, I planned my escape. I could jump on that tree and make it over the fence.
"I wouldn't think about that if I was you!" said a 300-pound white, bald man in scrubs.
I made a run for it anyway.
He yanked me down and yelled, "Get a strait jacket!" It took two guys to pin me down and secure the jacket on me.

I was tied up and brought inside to a white room with nothing in there but cameras and a mat. I began to tear the seams out of the mat with my teeth. They saw what I was doing from the spy room. Immediately a nurse who was laughing opened the door and snatched the mat from my jaws. All that was left was me and the cameras. I started feeling claustrophobic. My head and face itched, my back could use a scratch, and my hair found just the right place to stick itself in my eyes.

All I could do was roll around as if stuck in a wine barrel. That got the stray hairs out of my eyes. After ten minutes, I got quiet, and they let me out of the room and restraints. Weeks later when I was allowed outside again, the patients and I went for a smoke break. I turned the dial to the rock station on my headphones. The band Korn was on. I heard them before, but this time the ground shook beneath me. I stared at the sky. I noticed my arm had not throbbed in a while. I enjoyed the light breeze and I felt Korn sung directly to me.

One day, as I walked in line to lunch, I looked in a room. It was the conductor! The conductor of this train that I was in right now. He was in the same hospital from a decade ago. Now he's a conductor. Why? I wondered.

The conductor was wearing an orange short-sleeved prison jumpsuit like he was now with full-sleeved prison tats that were all faded black. He was something to look at. I could see he had a smirk beneath his dreads, and he was tall and skinny but fit with rough sundried skin.

He folded seemingly ironed clothes in his dresser neatly and with care like he was once in the military. The clothes were thick, orange and cotton, the same thing he wore in this train right now! I felt the conductor was a god.
The curtain closed.

Chapter 10

The curtain reopened.

My mom, uncle, and my sister each visited me separately in the hospital. I still thought I was special, but I was being drugged to be like everyone else. This hospital was beating me down. I wasn't all there mentally. I was a shell. I didn't remember conversations from my family visits, but I remember my family had been there. Sometimes it seemed like families lost hope or gave up on other patients because I never saw them being visited.

As I saw this in the train, I realized I was lucky to still have my family's support. Sometimes though, I wished my family never visited me at all.

I saw from the perspective on the train as it rolled by another scene, there was a meeting with the therapist from the governmental hospital joining troops with my family. The therapist's primary objective was to see if my family agreed with my release.

My eyes were hollow; why was it my family's decision if I stayed or left? The therapist spoke about her concerns with my uncle and mother. This counselor never looked at me. She educated my family about my diagnosis of bipolar I (one) schizoaffective disorder since I never experienced an episode before.

The therapist said it was like walking through a black labyrinth with the lights off trying to find some meaning in life. This maze goes on forever sometimes even when I stay on my meds. I fit the mold because it usually happens in the early 20's.

My uncle apparently had done some research through the web only to find some articles to explain my behavior. "Can drugs affect this?" my uncle asked the therapist.

"Drugs can exacerbate it, but it's already there. Do you guys have family members with a history of mental illness?" the therapist asked.

"Yes, my sister had it and so did my brother," my mom answered.

"And my uncle's mom was schizophrenic," I added.

"You don't know what you are talking about Lara," my uncle insisted. Apparently, he didn't want to admit what we all knew.

"So, why did she have electroshock therapy?" I asked as he fumed.

The therapist noticed my uncle's prejudice and saw how he believed he had to be right.

"You do not have to be on drugs to have a psychotic episode," the therapist intervened. "Your niece is schizoaffective as well as having a mood disorder. It's not uncommon to have these episodes even without trying a drug. Patients who have never smoked cigarettes before can have these delusions. Also, there are people who have had a lifetime full of drugs and never succumb to the disorder," she concluded.

"But everyone thinks I'm on drugs because they don't understand!" I exclaimed and looked at my uncle.

It took a month, but I was released. My mom's boyfriend Bill suggested that I move to their house and leave New York City in the past. "Go to school here," Bill said, "and heal." I still wanted to go back to NYC, but I listened to him.

I lived with my mom and Bill for two years after my episode. I was 25 years old when my second manic episode began. I didn't take meds at that time because all this insanity was done and over with, I thought. I'm normal, it was just a mental breakdown. Even Bill thought it was just a mental vacation from the heartache I had with Donny.

The curtain closed.

Chapter 11

The curtain reopened.

I was at my mom's house and heard on the radio a contest
for one lucky winner to go to Los Angeles to meet the band
Linkin Park and spend three days with them. This was my
favorite band!
I called and made it through the contest. I won!
I was so excited! I bought new clothes and cut my hair
choppy.
Four days before my meeting with Linkin Park, my mom
asked me if I was going to get up for school, I didn't answer.
She yelled, "OK, you're going to miss school!" and she left.
We carpooled together.
I was ecstatic! I couldn't wait for the concert and to finally
meet them.
That day I missed school, I had nowhere to go, but I was
going somewhere anyway. I was manic again, having my
second episode.
I threw on a dress, shawl, and sandals. I did not bother to
shower or shave, and I was awake for days.
I took to the streets.
On the access road, the minute I stuck my thumb out, I was
picked up by a trucker.
"Where you headed?" he asked.
"Iraq," I said, I thought I'd be back in time to see Linkin Park.
"Iraq?" he questioned.
"Yep." I affirmed.
"Iraq? Why?" he asked half-laughing.

"Going to fight in the war." I affirmed.

"Well, okay. I got a stop in Houston first to unload," he said sweetly.

I realized he wasn't taking me directly to the airport, but I knew he would after Houston.

As I sat in the back of the cabin, the trucker turned on the radio to my favorite rock station. I kept talking about the hair on my legs and he nicely covered them with a blanket. I needed to get dressed for the war I was going to fight in Iraq. I had money. I kept pressuring Harry, the driver, to stop at a clothing store.

Finally, we went to a thrift store. A female employee looked suspiciously at us, rather, suspiciously at the trucker. I gave her a hatred-filled look back. The trucker got us out of there in a hurry. He didn't like being watched.

On the road Harry filled up with gas at a truck stop. I got out and noticed the sun gleaming through his eyes; his chocolate skin glistened.

"You remind me of me," I said noticing his kind eyes.

Back in the truck, I sat feet up in the driver's seat, waiting for this guy to quit pumping gas. I put a cigarette in my mouth and the big ball of flame up in the sky was coming down to light it.

Once the trucker came back, the sun bounced off to the backdrop it once came from like a basketball. That experience was one reason I loved mania. Mania was the ultimate natural drug; it was two years since I did ecstasy or any drug. I then lit my own cigarette. Damn him for coming in and messing up my vision.

Harry stopped at the drop off station and unloaded.

"Ready?" the truck driver asked.

We got back in the truck.

He said he was tired, and that tomorrow was to be an all-nighter.

Later, he drove us to a convenience store, and we watched some television. I asked him to buy some tequila.

I'd been asking him for hours. "I have money. We can get the good stuff," I pleaded.

The trucker then went out and bought a liter of some cheap wine cooler stuff with my money and joined me back in the truck.

He took a few swigs then I took it. I gulped the rest of the liter without stopping. I was so thirsty. I hadn't had water in a while. The wine cooler was refreshing.

He looked at me, shocked.

I continued to laugh and watch television. I thought everything was about me. I thought the actors were talking about me or to me through the television with their jokes and sense of humor because it was like mine. They looked out directly through the television and saw me.

"Look, it's working," the trucker said. He was making his move to try to relate to me, but he didn't know crap about what I believed.

I just looked at him. How does he know anything? He doesn't, I thought.

Not one minute later, he tried to kiss me.

"No, you're just my friend," I said sweetly, pushing him back.

He came back and pulled down my dress enough to show my nipple.

He sucked it.

I kept pushing him away, more forcefully, but not enough to hurt him; he was my friend, or so I wanted to believe.

Once I realized this was bad, and it might not stop, I screamed, pleading with my whole heart. This can't happen.

I screamed a blood curdling scream.

I screamed so hard, someone had to hear. That was what I was relying on. It was as if I could see people coming to break down the door of the 18-wheeler.

I screamed. It wasn't going to stop.

I had never been raped before and this guy thought I was his property. He thought I had no rights. I wasn't even a human. I wasn't a person. That was the worst of it. I couldn't control what happened to me. He was going to take what he wanted. I was defenseless.

He hit me in the jaw and smothered me until I surrendered. I couldn't really fight him, not physically, he was too overpowering, but somehow, he continued to be my friend. I still saw the good in him. He didn't try to take away my freedom or life, he just took my body.

The number one thing I didn't want when I was manic was to be placed in a mental hospital where all my mental freedoms were prohibited. They'd drug you, abuse you, steal from you and keep you in for weeks to months.

Basically, if they kept you as a zombie, they did their job.

At the time, I was just confused as to why the trucker wanted to harm me. We were having such a good time. He was nice before. I couldn't control anything now.

He rolled me over and put his dick in me.

I still had my dress on. He just lifted it up.

I passed out. Thank you, higher gods!

While passed out, in my mind's eye, I heard the screams of my pregnant sister, Mom, and volunteers looking for me in the woods near my mom's house.

I could see my sister with no makeup on the news crying and praying for any leads to her missing sister. My sister, Darcy, was worried if I was cold or hungry. In my dream state I saw them searching in the pouring rain.

This was in my dream, but it was also a prophecy, and it really did happen. I found that out later. An old picture of me was on the news and my family was indeed looking for me.

The curtain closed.

Chapter 12

The curtain reopened.

The birds chirped and the warm sun shined on my face. It was a new day. I opened my eyes and was face to face with my nightmare. I clung to the sheets when I saw him staring at me. I wondered if Harry stared at me the whole night. When I passed out the night before, I still had my dress on, but now I was naked. What did he do to me?
I covered myself up shyly with the sheet. I felt confused and abused. I slept through the whole ordeal. I was so lucky! I didn't want to be conscious through that. That's probably what saved my life. I couldn't fight. He was going to get it regardless. It's hard to feel so helpless. It was out of my control what happened to my body, to my soul and mind.
I asked Harry to step out of the 18-wheeler because I had to get dressed.
I slipped on my dress, amazed I wasn't in a trash can.
I went outside and asked him if he wanted a beer; he opted out. He was still, in my mind, my friend.
I got my purse and went into the store.
His truck engine started. He was gone.
I needed something to drink.
Inside my purse all my money was gone. Hundreds of dollars gone; he stole it. He bought cheap liquor with my money last night and must have taken the rest.
The trucker left me stranded in another city; didn't he know there was nowhere for me to go?

There were men stocking beer at the back of the convenience store.

I moseyed in.

"You're not allowed in here," one said.

They looked at me like I was crazy.

Without money, I grabbed a beer.

"Don't you speak English? You're not allowed in here!" The other exclaimed.

I turned around, then dallied into the front door of the convenience store.

I snatched a beer and proceeded to the front door.

"Hey! Hey! You have to pay for that!" the clerk yelled. The customers were in shock.

Ok, time to leave. I put the alcohol down on the counter and walked out.

The teller called the cops anyway and a policeman was already waiting outside for me.

He was nice and asked me if I wanted to sit in the passenger's seat.

He had blonde hair and was very friendly.

"What's your name?" he asked.

"Marilyn Monroe," was my immediate response.

He giggled.

"What's your address?" he continued.

"524 Shuskaberry Lane," I said.

I made him chuckle. He did not charge me with anything, I was just strange and did nothing wrong. He was trying to figure me out; that was what it seemed.

I never told him about the truck driver. It wasn't even on my mind. The police officer did not handcuff me or put me in the backseat because I was just wacky, not a threat.

He still took me to the police station.

At the station he got out of the patrol car and talked to a policewoman.

I was still in the passenger side of the patrol car.

I carefully scooted over into the driver's seat.

There was no reading this cop's mind as to why he left the keys in the ignition, but who cares? I tried to drive away even though it was a cop car.

Both cops pulled out their guns.

I was sobered.

"Hands in the air! Hands in the air!" they both yelled.

It's no joke having a gun pointed at your face. I never thought I was going to die though.

I put my hands up, like they said, and got on the ground.

The male police officer picked me up and threw me against the wall.

They were arresting me for trying to steal a cop car.

The female officer frisked me, and then put me in handcuffs.

She weighed about 200 pounds with a bowl-style haircut.

"Is this the only way you can get a girl?" I yelled.

The curtain closed.

Chapter 13

The curtain reopened.

I was in jail.
Night came, lights off.
An officer threw blue rubber pads down, and the prisoners
scrambled like pigeons to grab dibs for a thin cushion.
I didn't care for the pad, they all had dibs anyway. It wasn't
like I was going to get one. Only a few were passed out.
It was extremely cold.
In my corner, I sat against the wall in the bathroom. I heard
18-wheelers rev up their engines and vibrate the wall.
"They're coming!"
"They're coming!" I exclaimed in my head. I'm being rescued
by rock stars in 18-wheelers.
I sat on the bathroom floor, a leaky showerhead with water
drip, drip, dripping on my head.
I kept saying, "And then, and then, and then".
I was imagining the book I was going to write. "And then this
happened, and then that happened. And then, and then,
and then," I kept this mantra going all night with drops of
water falling on my head.
"Shut up!" one of the inmates yelled at me.
I didn't listen.
Morning came.
"Ms. Monroe," said the officer clanking the door open,
"You're free to go," he said.
"How? Why?" I asked confused.
"Someone bailed you out," a cop said.

I thought it was my mom.

"These are the two who paid your bail." They were a black couple I had never seen before.

Well, whatever, I thought. I followed them out.

I never questioned why they bailed me out.

In the train, I remembered this scene. I could slightly recall seeing this black woman in the jail with me at some point. I was in a holding cell for only one day and night before being bailed out by the couple. I had brain fog though and the details of her in the cell with me at the time was distorted. The curtain closed.

Chapter 14

The curtain reopened.

I could barely fit in the car because it was so nasty cluttered with trash everywhere. Also, their seats were pushed back far. I wondered why they needed so much room, for how skinny they were.
They took me to a run-down house that looked like all the other dilapidated houses in the neighborhood.
I got out of the car and followed them inside. The woman left me alone to watch MTV. I laughed and laughed. I loved laughing. It was the high, a mania high.
The woman came in the room as night fell.
She suggested we should put my 14-karat gold Claddagh ring, a gift from my mom, in a baggy so I don't lose it.
She wanted to wash my hair in the sink, and she also wanted to shave my legs personally.
It felt weird. I told her I'd do it myself.
"Okay," she sweetly said and backed off.
I took a shower on my own and shaved.
She and I wore the same size pants, and she picked out some jeans for me. They were like country western pants, no pockets, striped Rocky Mountain jeans.
She led me by my hand into the other room where her husband laid on the couch.
She wanted to show him the pants she gave me. She spun me around to show off her handiwork.
"Doesn't she look good in this? Look at her butt!" she showcased me to her husband.

I felt weird again.

The moon was up, and I had things to do.

"I got to go; they are calling me!" I said speaking of an urge in my being.

The man rose from the couch and forcefully said, "No, you're staying with us!"

He pushed me against the wall.

I had no idea who these people were, but in mania, I was like a child. I trusted everyone until my gut said to go. This couple obviously wanted to take advantage of me. They were just waiting until nightfall. My bail must not have been that high.

Suddenly, just by this, I felt violated again! I couldn't control my own body or will!

"This is a bad neighborhood; you're not going anywhere!" he exclaimed.

This man obviously didn't get what I was saying in English, so I tried a new way. I spoke Snoop Dogg to him. "For shizzle dazzle my triple dimple, shiva daddle, you follow!" That was how I heard Snoop Dogg talk on MTV earlier. His new frame of rap jive.

"You are!" he replied.

"Yes, I am!" He finally realized I'm God.

"We got to take you somewhere," he said.

I was cool with that. I forgot to get my Irish ring that she had put in a baggy. We were out of that stinky, cluttered, dump.

They took me to the police department, right up the road, again.

I got out and they took off.

Houston must be full of jerks who just take you somewhere and drive off like the truck driver.
I went inside and asked the lady at the front desk of the police department if they had any tequila.
I never told on the couple, nor that Harry raped me.
The curtain closed outside on the subway platform.

Chapter 15

The curtain reopened.

A police officer took me to the mental hospital after I asked
for some alcohol.
I was clinked in. I did the drill. I unlaced my shoelaces for the
hospital staff for fear of me committing suicide or choking
someone else to death. They also put my personal
belongings in a paper bag. Hopefully I'd get it back.
My arm was pulsing with the GPS tracker Donny put in it.
"Donny, Donny!" I kept asking, crying, and exclaiming.
The nurse looked like Donny.
"You got super tall! Don't leave me, Donny. Stay with me," I
begged.
The nurse seemed to feel my pain. He looked like he wanted
to help. But he didn't know what to do so he only did what
he was taught.
He shot me in the butt with a large needle. It was a medicine
that was supposed to calm me down. I didn't know what
was in the syringe. It left me even more dazed, dizzy, and
confused for three days.
The doctor smothered the symptoms as he overmedicated
me. That was why I was able to leave so soon.
Around the time I was scheduled to leave, a sleazy doctor
came in with my mom.
I wouldn't look at my mom or talk to her.
The sleazy doctor looked at my chest and determined I had
lost weight.
I was pissed.

He was a doctor. He had no right to use his status to check out my breast size.

He claimed that I showed my breasts in the men's unit.

"Well, maybe you shouldn't have drugged me up so much! You're the culprit, not me; I don't even remember that shit!" I swore.

My mom looked sad and believed him. She always listened to doctors over me; she's a nurse. Once I was released, my uncle wanted to see me back in San Antonio.

We went to my sister, Darcy's house.

Darcy took a picture of my uncle and me. He was hugging me, but I had a smirk on my face and was crouched over covering my breasts over my shirt.

They knew something was wrong although I didn't tell them about the rape or anything. When I was manic, I didn't give a fuck about my family nor childhood friends. I hated them all. There was more to this world than their physical "reality". They could not accept my brain nor how it worked. I did not want any part of them telling me what I see, hear, and think is not real. I was gifted, not a druggie. I dared anyone to test me for drugs.

A week after my release from the hospital in Houston, I was still manic, but no one could tell. I got good at acting well. The curtain closed.

Chapter 16

The curtain reopened.

Once back at my mom's house, I cranked the radio full blast.
My mom came in several times pleading for me to turn the
radio down. She and Bill had to get up for work early in the
morning. Finally, Bill came in and tore the cord out of the
radio and aimed it towards my head. He didn't hit me, but
he pushed me on the bed, not hard though; he held back. I
sprang right back up and stared him straight in the eye.
"You're not in control of me. I can fight you and I am not
scared!" I exclaimed.
"That's it, you're going to the hospital!" He said the worst
words I never wanted to hear. He picked me up in his arms
and carried me down the stairs. Wearing my combat boots, I
scuffed the walls as much as I could. "You are not my
father," I yelled. I wanted to spit and spread venom. I
wanted to hurt and spread pain. I wanted to be free. I saw
things others couldn't. I knew all the answers and I could see
visions others wouldn't dare. My mom rushed me into the
hospital. She was grabbing my arm panicking. Her hand felt
like a cold wrench as she hurried me towards the front desk.
I tried to hit her. Several nurses ran to her aid. My mom was
afraid for my safety and afraid of this person I'd become. I
was sure she wondered if I would ever return to my happy,
giving, sweet self. In fact, my whole family said I'd never
come back and end up in an institution for the rest of my
life. My mom would fight to the end for me, but at the time,
I thought she was taking away my freedom.

Her eyes were watery, and she was without makeup. She was rarely seen in public without makeup unless it had to do with getting me help. She needed to wake up at 4:30 a.m. to go to work, but I remembered she was there, in that cold, chilly hospital, with bloodshot eyes in the middle of the night with me.

My mom was closed in an office talking to the doctor with plexiglass separating us. The doctor took notes. I yelled that my mom was a whore with straw-like hair. Her hair was all messed up. Normally her hair was a style of her personality, perfect. I yelled without truth. "Whore, whore, whore!" My mom was always happy or sad because of me. I wanted to see her erupt. I wanted to see her pain, her core! I was trying to hurt her.

She cried when she saw my hatred for her, and I could tell what she felt in her heart as she slumped. The nurse got a needle, pulled down my pants in front of other patients. I fought, but in the needle plunged.

Some of the patients looked at me, some of them were glued to the TV and whispered or laughed out loud hysterically. A few of them cried and others moaned and drooled along their shirts as they slept. It was a packed house.

The curtain closed.

The conductor in the subway train slowed down and I could see the reflection of my own appearance through the plexiglass. I looked like a guy on drugs, but I wasn't. I was wide-eyed and ugly. I was not the Greek goddess I once thought I was in other episodes. Then he started the train again to the next station. Once again, a scene from my past flashed before me.

Chapter 17

The curtain reopened.

I quit college, moved out, and began stripping again. This time at Private Garden Strip Club, where Bobo worked as a DJ.
We had a friendship until I moved to New York City before my first episode began. He was my first true crush. When I walked into the club, I was happy to see him there. My feelings for Bobo never left.
Not long after seeing Bobo again, we began dating for the first time. I thought New York was the best time of my life. Bobo lived his early life in the country. He rode tractors and created food plots. He was a country guy at heart. He was the opposite of Donny. Bobo smoked weed, listened to Bob Marley, Jimmy Hendrix, and metal from the eighties like Iron Maiden, and Judas Priest.
The owners of Private Garden let Bobo tend to their ranch on weekends.
The images I saw outside the train window brought back good memories of us. I remembered what it was like in the early days at the ranch with Bobo. It beat out all the times I spent with anyone else.

Bobo and I used to set traps for wild boars to control the population. There were too many of these wild pigs. We snared several; we did that every night and then usually he'd kill it with a gun. One night he handed me his Colt 44 Magnum and said, "Okay, now you're going to put the crosshairs in the middle of his ..." Bang, I killed it right between the eyes before he finished his sentence.

"How'd I do?" I asked wide eyed. Bobo laughed and said, "You did it like a country girl surprisingly".

"I'm good with guns," I said.

In the train, I missed Bobo. I treated him badly and left him like he was nothing, like he was insignificant and had no home with me.

There were so many good times with Bobo. Like when I threw rocks out of the food plots only wearing combat boots and a sunburn. It was deep country, so no one drove by or could see.

One day, Bobo did a wheelie on the ATV and I fell backwards dangling off the back. My back dragged across the dirt and rocky ground as I held onto the back rail. I thought I could pull myself back up. Bobo looked at the shadow of us to see how high his wheelie was. He looked at my shadow and all he could see was feet straight up in the air. He turned around and saw me skidding on the dirt and rocks. I was so embarrassed.

"Let go!" he yelled. That day I was wearing a yellow shirt, daisy dukes with no panties. I let go and when he turned around all he saw was dirt gathered all around and inside my daisy dukes. Bobo loved to tell stories about us to his friends. For instance, one night while snaring wild boars, Bobo caught one and used his bow and arrow to kill it. He hit the boar, and all I heard was a loud angry squeal of the 260-pound boar. I took off, away from the sound. It was around 3 a.m. and I didn't have a flashlight. I ran straight into the heart of a bunch of cacti. I didn't miss a beat but kept jumping, running, and falling into one cactus after another. Later Bobo plucked cactus needles out of my butt and intimates for over an hour.

A few months down the road, Bobo got a manager position in a Dallas strip club. He moved and I was sad because I lived six hours away. I wanted to follow him there.

I visited him one day in Dallas and we got high, out in the open on The Grassy Knoll in sight of where JFK got shot. We also went through the museum about the conspiracy and whether Lee Harvey Oswald was the only shooter or not. We agreed, what a crock.

Again, while we drove to dinner, Bobo lit one up. He passed it to me and asked how I liked it. "Well, I like it, but I don't like it," I said.

"That's dirt weed, it does that to everyone," he said. At that we both laughed our asses off.

There were other short memories of our time together, that in a way of remembering, kept our life cute. He would often recall moments we shared that made him laugh.

One memory was when he snuck around a dark corner while I was brushing my teeth. He loves to tell that story. He sneaked out of a dark corner and screamed at me. I would start high stepping in place with toothpaste flying everywhere as I screamed, and he giggled.

Back in the train, I was remembering and seeing the memories of my life.

I moved to Dallas to be closer to Bobo. I stayed at my cousin's house.

My cousin was so ecstatic I was living with him. "Drink as much wine as you want!" My cousin Trey was making payments on a nice house in suburbia. He hadn't met his neighbors yet, but he would, and everyone would be happy to know each other. That's what I gathered. He had dark wood floors and a bar in the kitchen. Everything was tidy. I liked staying with him.

I drank, and drank, and drank my cousin's wine. I drank at least a bottle a night.

I danced in Dallas too. My cousin didn't mind, mostly because he had opened his mind to the idea. I drank so much at work that I'd have to pull over, sleep, and vomit in my own truck until daylight came.

Usually, I'd talk to Bobo every day. But I texted him without any reply for about five days. My arm started throbbing again. It was Donny, calling for my attention. The implant pulsated its signal to me.

It seemed Bobo didn't care about my outreach; he never replied. My mind automatically went to a sore spot within my soul. I was sure he was cheating. I pretended not to care. For two weeks, I was stressed and became manic once again.

I watched TV for twenty-four hours without sleep. When Bobo finally called after two weeks, I declined the call. Tommy Lee was on The Tonight Show, and I projected a thought, "Lick Eva Longoria's face!" She was the first guest. With some hesitation, he did lick her face. "That's it! Famous people, especially rock stars, know who I am and can read my thoughts. Proof!" I knew.

The curtain closed.

Chapter 18

The curtain reopened.

The sun would rise, the sun would fall, and once again I was in my room laughing hysterically at the TV.
My cousin, Trey came in and I acted like a valley girl when I spoke to him.
"You've been cooped up in your room, Lara, for weeks. Everything okay?"
"Yeah, I'm fine. Like, Bobo hasn't called me in two weeks." I twisted my hair. "But, like, Donny wants my attention every day," I giggled.
"What do you mean? That guy from New York? Lara, he married someone else," Trey said.
"Yeah, but he implanted a needle in my arm, a tracking device," I said.
"I think you're going manic, Lara. I'm going to call your mom!"" he said. "No more wine," he continued.
Trey got on the phone with my mom, and I knew I had to get out of there. They're going to lock me up. I'll be in for months, I thought. A storm was coming in. I must leave. I got in my truck as pebbles of rain hit my windshield.

I drove uphill, offroad, up and down through bumps and turns in my little Ford Ranger pickup. I found some grass and parked. My radio was blasting to the frequency matching my feelings of rage and heartbreak; the dial was set to hard rock music. I listened to the song "Before I Forget" by the band Slipknot. I took out a cigarette and lit it, the rain was not too bad now. I could still light it up. The crackle of thunder roared in the distance. I kneeled outside my truck and dropped to my knees and prayed. I don't know why I was praying; I was God, after all, in all my madness.

My forearm throbbed.

The police drove up.

I hated police. They always took me to the hospital.

"Do you know you're trespassing?" the mean one asked.

"No," I answered.

"There are signs all over the place," the other cop said.

"What are you smoking?" the speculative dick asked.

"Cigarettes," I answered.

"More like ciga-weed," the dick said. "She's on drugs or something!" he continued.

"No, I'm not! Test me!" I yelled as I stuck out my arm so angry.

The nice cop said, "We'll give you a chance. Is there someone you can call to get you out of this mess? Someone who can tow your truck too?"

"Yes." I was relieved I had a reason to call Bobo.

"If he doesn't answer, we're taking you to jail," the mean fat one stated.

I called Bobo from my phone. "Please answer Bobo!" I prayed. He answered! Self-conscious and manic, I didn't make sense to Bobo on the other line.

The nice policeman put his hand out for me to give him the phone. He introduced himself to Bobo and said I was trespassing in an oil field.

I heard Bobo on the phone saying, "She's bipolar and is probably going through an episode".

Bobo drove up about twenty minutes later in his Land Rover and hugged me. He looked very concerned.

We got everything lined up and Bobo took me back to my cousin's house. Bobo and Trey met for the first time. My cousin said I had to go to the hospital. Bobo suggested calling an ambulance, so I'd be more comfortable. Bobo and Trey followed behind the ambulance.

I made the paramedics laugh hysterically. "Why is Britney Spears famous?" I cackled. "It's not like she writes her own songs, and if she does, they suck," I said. The whole ride was about Britney Spears. All the paramedics circled around me as if we were hanging out at a campfire and I was the entertainment. I was strapped in a gurney at the time.

"Is Bobo still behind us?" I asked.

"Yes, he won't leave you," one of the paramedics said.

"Good. I hope he follows us the whole way to the hospital." I was afraid he'd leave me like everyone else had.

We got to the hospital and Bobo waited for me outside the ambulance, ready to hold my hand.

"Why were you talking about that pop star the whole time? You don't even know her!" Bobo asked confused when the paramedics dropped me off at the hospital.

The paramedics told him. Why? Isn't a patient's info supposed to be private? I thought.

My cousin had to go to work; Bobo said he'd wait for me to get signed into the mental hospital. The only reason I surrendered to this idea was because Bobo was with me.

The lobby was full of people and their families.

Bobo held my hand as I squeezed it the entire time.

Around three hours later, the doctor came out and asked me if I wanted Bobo to come in seeing that he was already following behind me.

"Yes! Oh yes!" I nodded.

"So, Lara, who is this?" The doc asked.

"This is my boyfriend, Bobo." I answered.

"So, why are you here today, Lara?" the doctor continued.

"To support the medical community," I said with certainty.

Bobo laughed, and the doctor looked confused.

When the doctor's evaluation was over and I was admitted, Bobo went back to work. The nurses led me towards the ward.

There were at least 40 patients waiting for a bed. It was like a Saturday church slumber party for kids. It was packed with patients sitting on the ground, telling stories even if just for themselves. Some writing, some drawing, some coloring.

Look! – there was Jesus, the Virgin Mary, Mary Magdalen and oh no! Judas!

As far as I could tell, all the patients and I had a few things in common; we wanted to play outside and be free to be who we believed we were. Also, it would seem, no matter how powerful, could escape the governmental control that kept us in these hospitals.

Some of us could have faked it out of there though. You know, faked a smile, kept track of the dates, and participated in group sessions. Faking it was hard for me though because I hated people, and I didn't want to be someone else. In court, where they decide if they keep you in the hospital longer, I always blew it.

They'd ask what I wanted to do when I got out and this time I said, "I will go to Africa and learn the dancing styles there and teach," I answered their questions truthfully. Wrong answer.

"I can see you are still grandiose, Lara, so we are going to have to keep you another week," the judge stated.

Before I was out of the court, I yelled, "It's my dream! How dare you for punishing me for having a dream!"

My doctor at this hospital left me so medicated that I slept for a few days, only to be awoken to eat and stand in the medication line to eventually get my meds.

A few weeks later, I was back at my cousin's house.

I didn't think anyone knew that I was still manic. I sat in my room all day. Doing the same thing, watching TV, and laughing hysterically.

Bobo called at least three times a day. He was worried. His love surprised me. I never knew a man to love me so much the way he did.

Bobo came over one night. He took me to Sonic and bought us both jalapeno poppers. Then we went back to my cousin's. "You got to get all this bad energy out of you. Here, run up this hill as fast as you can. It'll help," Bobo suggested. That was interesting because all the psychiatric doctors said similar things.

"I used to be in track, so I'm fast," I prepared him.

We spread apart.

Clump, clump, clump, clump. My feet were held down by invisible bricks. I swear, they were heavy! "I'm faster than that!" I exclaimed.

Bobo laughed, "You're a little faster running from a boar then ending up in cacti!" he joked.

He gave me a hug and told my cousin we were getting a hotel and would spend the week there.

Bobo and I stocked up on groceries as he held my hand. I loved going to the grocery store with him. Being with him was home.

After that, Bobo and I went to a hotel to stay for a bit and heal in his care. The first night, I kept laughing hysterically at the TV. During the movie, I saw butt loads of naked men running into the ocean. Bobo later asked me what I was laughing at, and I told him.

"That's a hallucination, Donkis," (that was his nickname for me). "It wasn't in the movie." Bobo concluded and went to sleep while I tried to not laugh too loud at the movie.

Bobo still went to work every night while I stayed in the hotel. He called and checked on me every few hours.

One day, Bobo had to work an eighteen-hour day. I was hungry and went to Denny's across the street. The people there looked at me strangely. I felt like I looked like a Greek goddess even though I hadn't slept or showered in over a week and maybe even stunk. At Denny's the mashed potatoes tasted like the best vanilla ice cream anyone ever tasted. When manic, food tasted magical.

Unfortunately, we only rented the room for a week, and I had to go back to my cousin's.

Trey was concerned again. I did nothing but stay in the room and laugh at the TV. Knock, bang, knock, bang. Trey could not stop interrupting my conversation with the TV. I planned it, one more knock or barge in and I'm going to make him wish he never opened the door again.

My cousin barged in again!

I threw off my yellow hockey jersey to show my naked body. I spread my legs and dared him to come into the room some more.

"You're sick, Lara!" He judged me and closed the door. That was exactly what I wanted him to do. CLOSE THE DOOR AND LEAVE ME THE FUCK ALONE!

As soon as he left, I put the jersey back on, rolled my eyes, and picked up a book to read. He wouldn't be coming in again. I was sure of that.

He called my mom.

My mom's boyfriend, Bill, had his own plane and flew Mom to Dallas the next day. She took a week off from work.

"Lara, you need to take your meds." My mom said once at my cousin's. I walked to the other room. She brought in my meds, separated them, and counted them out. She was a panicky mess with a soft yell as far as her voice would go. I ignored her. She held them out and got juice and threatened to call the hospital again. I took my meds.

My cousin came home and the sight of him made me mad. He had underlying judgement and said I was sick and needed to be exorcised. He said over and over I was possessed. I ripped off my clothes again and ran outside naked just to piss him off and to give the neighbors something to talk about. He tackled me and brought me back inside.

I grabbed his cherrywood clock and thrashed it along his dark hardwood floors. The wood gave way and cracked. Then I flicked a lighter to his wall and said I'd catch the place on fire. I got close and he tackled me again. My mom and Trey threatened me again with hospitalization. I lied and said I'd put on my clothes and agreed to go to the hospital. I changed into army pants and a black top with combat boots and snuck past them. I ran down the street.

My cousin was getting sick of me; but he managed to give me chance after chance.

I was going to the local airport down the street to get something to eat.

Apparently, my cousin called the cops on me because an officer pulled up and tried to get my attention.

"Excuse me, ma'am. Excuse me! Where are you going?" he asked.

I didn't know it was illegal to ignore an officer, so I just kept walking.

He jumped out of his car and put his hands around my waist while I kicked and screamed. I threw up on his shoes out of disturbance to my freedom. "How could he touch me?" I thought. "I did nothing wrong!" The rage started to creep up inside me. Approaching cars slowed down for the spectacle. They were all googly eyed, probably never having seen such a thing in their quiet suburbia neighborhood.

He called the scoundrels that got me in this mess, my mom and Trey. They dropped all charges and asked him to let me go. He told me "You're lucky to have such a nice, understanding family." I didn't believe him.

My cousin told me to get my stuff and go. I packed my truck with as much as I could and headed back to San Antonio.

I arrived back in San Antonio and found an apartment quickly. I returned to stripping to keep the bills paid.

My manic episode stopped about a week after arriving back in San Antonio.

As fate would have it, Bobo was called back to San Antonio to work, and I was thrilled by the news.

We moved in together. I never felt something better in my life. After Bobo moved back, he asked me to marry him. I was so ecstatic, "Yes!" I wanted a baby, he didn't. One day frolicking in the closet, he said, "Let's have a baby!" I never imagined a baby who could be cuter, and I never imagined a better father. He wanted a baby to show his love for me.

I loved watching movies with him, and I enjoyed waking him up for the good parts. "You're missing it! This is the good part!"

I loved it when he would get on the couch naked with me and I would hold him, all of him. It made us vulnerable to each other.

We would go to the movies with his daughter, Kelly. All of us would smoke weed outside the theatre.

Bobo and I had so many adventures. One day, Bobo was lancing the venom of a brown recluse spider that bit my butt. It was painful "No more!" I screamed. "No more!" He got it all out and flicked it with his fingers. It hurt so bad, and in that moment, he reminded me of all my exes who aimed to hurt me.

He saw the look on my face that oozed, how could you hurt me? Tears streamed down my face, and I fell to the ground. He immediately kneeled on the ground where I was and said he was sorry. I replied, "This is all I ever wanted!" (Meaning the relationship we had together).

Bobo was on his knees rocking, holding me, as we both cried, "This is all I ever wanted, too," he said. This is my best memory of us. It's all I ever wanted.

There was one time when Bobo thought that I should go to school as a court reporter. I did not want to, but I did it to please him. Bobo bragged to all his friends about how well I was doing. He was so proud. But I am a creative person; I felt incredibly stifled going through something so boring as typing. At the same time, I kept pushing for Bobo to get a job, any job other than being a DJ. I was jealous of the girls who hung on him night after night in the DJ booth.

Doing something so sedentary was driving me crazy though and I soon became unhappy. I had never learned how to communicate in a relationship. I didn't want to disappoint Bobo and live through the torture of him not being proud of me. I didn't want him to think I was a loser. His approval was vital to me.

I broke up with Bobo. He got a job at an oil rig as a roughneck the day after we broke up. He had been applying for months. He never abandoned me when I was unkind. Yet, I abandoned him.

I decided to move out, and the days I packed we still slept in the same bed. He tried to cuddle, and I rolled over, giving him the cold shoulder. I don't know if he slept, but I could hear him cry every night and I could see him wipe his tears away.

As I drove off to leave him a few days later, he scrunched his face and begged the word, "Please!" That one moment haunted me on this road to Hell.

I saw my reflection in the train again. For the first time, I started crying. His desperate "Please," and his face clearly exposed his pain. Seeing his face and eyes again, so freshly hurt, killed me.

I wanted to turn my truck around and ease his pain. It hurt. But I had made my decision so I couldn't go back. Little did I realize I could. We could fix it all with communication.

Once again, I moved in with my parents. My mom pushed for me to get a job as a receptionist. Bobo called at night while I was at work and talked about us and I felt his pain but didn't care. How could I go back to Bobo with all this help from family? I thought, torn.

Bill also pulled some strings and got me a better, full-time job as a receptionist at a real estate company.

Over the course of six or seven months, Bobo called every day. "I am your friend, Lara, I will never let you go!" he said. "Well, I don't want to be your friend!" I snapped and the phone fell silent, "Well, I'll never call you back then, Lara. Goodbye," I heard him sniffle as he said that.

I felt cold and my stomach dropped, but I thought over meant over. I couldn't leave my family after all they had done for me. I knew Bobo still loved me. I wouldn't allow myself to go back because I cared too much of what my family thought. They helped move me out of Bobo's. They supported me in leaving the relationship because I felt like I had to be someone I wasn't. I was expected to be a court reporter and smile all the time to show Bobo I was happy. At least I thought that's what Bobo expected from me.

I was also very insecure. I thought he wouldn't like my real self, the self that needed space, and not be around him 24/7 nor be around his friends that much. It wasn't that I didn't like him or his friends. It was just that I was an introvert and had social anxiety. I felt I couldn't deny Bobo anything. So, I carried a smile on my face everywhere we went like a painted doll's face.

The curtain closed.

Chapter 19

The curtain reopened.

On the platform of the subway, an image materialized of Bobo's daughter, Kelly, and me at a restaurant.
I loved her and just wanted to talk. We talked about Bobo, mostly about his faults in the relationship. She listened and sympathized.
Bobo called when Kelly and I were having drinks. We met with him for lunch. He didn't know I would be there. Still, I had butterflies. I hadn't seen him in a year or so. The last thing I said to him was I didn't want to be his friend. Maybe that had been untrue.
Bobo was surprised to see me. His tender look showed his sadness.
At the table, he automatically moved to sit next to me. Kelly motioned him to sit next to her.
There was silence as the three of us ate. After lunch, I hugged Bobo to say goodbye and he asked with tears in his eyes if I was going to ride back with him. I saw his pain and agreed to go with him. This started our relationship again after a year, out of the blue.
I got into Bobo's truck and left Kelly to drive herself alone. I was all around confused.
I thought Kelly was confused too. I can't forget her face of "What the fuck?" Especially after all we just talked about.
Bobo and I slept together in his house that day. I knew him; he showed his feelings through sex.

Since then, Bobo and I secretively saw each other. I was paranoid someone would find out. He held out his hand for me to grab it at the store and I pushed it back. I was paranoid, I'd run into family and let them down. I feared my family giving up on me. They helped me live with them again only for me to be flaky and go back with Bobo.

Bobo always wanted to hold hands, kiss and cuddle after intimacy and liked to see my eyes sparkle like before as he was courting me for this second time.

Bobo's constant sensitivity and sincerity was apparent; I wanted another chance just like he did.

I changed my mind and became more affectionate. On my lunch break from work, I would visit Bobo at his house or a pancake restaurant. He was home to me. His body heat when he hugged me was home to me. He was the most grounded man I ever met in my life. That was so attractive to my flightiness, like order balancing my chaos.

Over and over, I told Bobo that if he let me move in, "It'd be different". He was reluctant, but his heart won out and I moved in for the second time.

Bobo wanted me to stay with a real job as a receptionist, but I thought the women in the office were out to get me.

Because of this paranoia, I quit the position immediately and I started stripping again.

The curtain closed.

Chapter 20

The curtain opened outside the train to me picking out paint
with a girl from the club, Martha, while at Lowes.

"What do you think would look good?" I asked her. "See, I'd
pick out bright yellow paint for the kitchen walls," I mused.
"When I first moved in, I wanted to redecorate everything,
but Bobo just said I could only do whatever I wanted to the
guest bathroom. Just the guest bathroom! The rest had to
be country, like him. The walls were pretty much bare
except that which he called, 'The Wall of Shame', and deer
heads."
"What's the wall of shame?" she giggled.
"He has a bunch of pictures of all the close people in his life.
He hung around bikers, and his uncle was in a biker gang
growing up, so he had lots of pictures of them," I said
grinning. "I guess we should stick to neutrals,".
"Got it," she concluded.
We picked out burnt orange, brown, and beige. I wanted to
surprise him when he came back from the rig.
We managed to only have time to paint the dining room
area brown, under the stairs neutral, and half of the living
room burnt orange. The house was large with three
bedrooms in an upscale neighborhood.
The night before he came home, I cut my shoulder-length
blonde hair into a bob and cried when the hairdresser
puffed it up. I looked like my mom. I hated her hair. Too
Southern. I also tried to do a mad dash to get all his laundry
done. It was loads of last-minute washing and drying.

The night he returned, I heard Bobo's black, muddy, diesel truck pulled up in the drive. I raced downstairs to get him a glass of ice with Jack Daniels in it and a straw.

I opened the door with a smile and with his drink in hand before he could get the keys in the lock.

"Your hair!" he said smiling.

"I know, I hate it!" I said tearing up.

"No, I love it!" he said, giving me a hug.

"What's this?" he looked down at the drink.

"It's for you," I said. "It's Jack on ice."

"Oh, alright," he said.

We went in.

I smiled at the beige under the stairs.

"You painted?" he said.

"Do you like it?" I asked.

"Yeah, it's alright," he said. "The baby poop color has got to go though," he said as we sat on the couch looking at my paint job.

"That doesn't look like baby poop," I said.

"You don't have kids," he stated blankly.

We both laughed.

The curtain closed.

Chapter 21

The curtain reopened.

Bobo and I each had our faults still. One day, the sun glared
through my sunglasses, and I was nursing a major hangover.
At the club the night before, I drank more than ten shots of
overpoured Patron with customers and my bare-breasted
friends.
From the train, I saw myself rolling around between the
frayed threads of the grey-brown comforter and rushing to
the bathroom, swallowing puke all the way.
The image was so clear when Bobo asked a friend from the
club to join us at Hooters. I heard him on the phone as I
rushed to the bathroom again. In between spewing, I turned
my head to catch his eye shaking my head "no" violently. I
looked in the mirror as my puke episode subsided and saw
busted red blood vessels under my eyes from straining my
throat, my lips quivering. I did not want to go.
"Bobo, I'm sick. I can't go!"
All he had to say was "for me?" and I went.
The logos on the tee-shirts of the girls at Hooters were owls.
These owls' eyes were poking out of their outfits as they
bounced across the too bright, too gleaming for my
hangover, light wood floors.
I wore my big-looking, owl-eyed shades as Bobo and his
friend ogled the girls.
"Ugh!" I was pissed and disgusted even though I was a
stripper and former Hooter's girl myself.

Bobo and his friend ordered spicy wings. I couldn't eat, especially spicy food, and no beer either.

I was quiet and from this train I was on with the conductor, I saw my head hanging low at the table at Hooters.

I waited uncomfortably.

We finally left.

At that time in my life, I was a nonsmoker and I told Bobo to not smoke in my truck. We were in my truck, and he lit up a cigarette anyway. "I told you not to smoke in my truck!" I pointed it out. He didn't care and stomped on the brakes. "Bobo, it makes me sick!" I stated again. *"Please,"* I scrunched my face and begged.

We were at a stop sign when I spewed all over the seat. I opened the door and the vomit exploded. I wasn't done. "There are cars behind us, Lara; I got to go," He explained why he had to take off and why I had to shut the door as we raced onto the highway.

I kept on puking, soaking my jeans.

"Roll down the window, Lara!" he screamed.

I puked out the window as he continued to smoke. We sped and I vomited all over the side of my truck as the wind carried it, all through my then blonde hair.

We rushed to Private Garden. Bobo was still a roughneck at the oil rig, but he was friends with the owner at the club and he wanted me to go inside with him!

"No way! I have puke all over my jeans and hair, Bobo!" I pleaded again because he always wanted to be around me and, sometimes, I needed my space. And I was I no condition to be out in public!

Days later, I would call every guy and girl I knew to complain. They pretty much all said the same thing, "Leave him."

Bobo called me while he was at work. I was watching TV in bed. I bitched to him that day and every day for the next week.

"This is the last time I'm going to say sorry, Lara," he apologized. "I know you're going to leave me," he concluded.

It was only six months into this second attempt at being together and when he said those words it made me realize, "Yeah, why am I staying?" I wasn't thinking about it, at all, before he said that.

I started moving my things shortly after that.

The furniture, pots, pans, and TVs were Bobo's. All that was left was the smell of his Marlboro Lights and my clothes. Bobo came in and saw me filling up plastic bags with the rest of my belongings.

"I just gotta get this," he said solemnly, "and then I'll leave you alone."

He reached for the African wall mask I bought him for Christmas one year and put it under his arm then left. His eyes weren't teary like the first time, just dead.

He moved out too. There were so many memories in that stained and half-painted house. He was getting some distance.

I rented an expensive townhouse with a garage.

I didn't care about the love I had with Bobo. I was done. Just like that I turned my feelings for Bobo off the moment I left.

I continued to strip. Bobo would come into the club when I worked during his weeks off from the rig to visit the owner. He'd look and stare at me giving dances to other guys. I didn't even say hi to him. I was annoyed; I had no feelings whatsoever. I knew he rode his motorcycle there. The scar on my knee should have reminded me of the motorcycle accident we had two years previous. We hit a deer head on going about 60-miles-an-hour. I remembered, he thought we were missing our ribs because the ribs we bought to cook were out of its saddlebag and busted out of their plastic. They were laying there among all the debris from the wreck.

Disoriented, Bobo's CD player was still playing Iron Maiden's song *The Number of the Beast.* Just as the chorus played, he looked towards the East where the big, blazing, orange sun was coming up over the hills. He thought we were dead, and the Devil was coming for us.

We should be bound by that accident. He almost died, and it didn't compute how hurt he was even when he was air lifted to the hospital.

In the accident, I shot off the bike like a lucky leprechaun, only fracturing my left knee. Bobo tried to save his bike and in doing so one lung was punctured and he had six broken ribs, a broken collarbone, and a broken shoulder blade. He also had two exposed kneecaps and a concussion. The nurse told the doctors she didn't think he would make it the first two hours. Bobo's daughter Kelly visited him and gave him a grave, terrified look that made him choose to fight. He survived.

From the scene of the accident a passerby drove us to a place where we would get an airlift for Bobo. It was a place close to our mutual friends, Clayton, and Candy.

The voice inside the train said, *"Like Hell you cared! Like an idiot, you didn't get it! You saw him in shock, passing out and blood oozing out of his ears. What did you do in that truck ride to the airlift pickup?"*
"I fucking talked him through the whole fucking thing. I prohibited him from falling asleep!" I yelled.
"Yeah, bitch, you talked about work! Even the driver looked at you in disbelief," the voice said.
"I didn't know how to care for someone hurt, okay? All I knew was to keep him conscious," I snapped.
The curtain closed.

Chapter 22

The curtain reopened.

After the Hooter's incident and after our second breakup, Christmas came. I worked for days making a game for my nieces and nephew to find gifts in a scavenger hunt. I became manic with this obsession. I stayed up for days focusing and buying supplies to make it fun for them, but they never experienced this game because I was still manic on Christmas day.

In my truck, I accidentally jumped a curb on the access road going to my family's place.

I called my mom's boyfriend Bill and told him I had a flat tire. I asked if he could help. I also called mutual friends of Bobo and mine. They all came.

The sun glared off their glasses and they looked like terminator cops. I was in trouble.

Bill found my spare and saw all the gifts I bought. I bought a children's drum set for my nephew, a beginner's guitar for my oldest niece, and musical hand shakers for my youngest niece. We all followed Bill's lead to my mom's house after he put the spare on.

Back in the train, I re-experienced my contempt for my mom's house. It had a country star of Texas on the front of the garage. They opened the gate that I was prohibited from knowing the code to; I guess that was because when I was manic, I was a threat. I did always misbehave when I was manic.

We went in. They had plantation shutters and the backyard seemed endless with deer roaming the property. It was not homey nor welcoming. The floors were so shiny, and everything was in its place. It appeared like no one lived in it.

Candy and Clayton, the friends I had also called to help fix the flat tire, entered. They were country folk. Real country folk who had tigers, mountain lions, and bears for pets, no shit!

Since I had spent days without sleeping, my mom gave Candy and me some tea with honey. Not a chance this was going to work; I mean are you kidding? I drank it, and then asked for wine.

"That's not good for your condition," my mom said. She gave in and poured me a glass anyway. "Just one," she said. The wine tasted like gold! I was royal. My mom asked what gold tastes like, and I said, "Like I was not born in Heaven, but in divine with rock stars". They looked at me like I made no sense.

Candy asked if I wanted to go with them to their little house in the country. I was afraid they'd see me if I did, the real me, the me that hated people. "It's okay, I'm leaving here and going back to my home shortly," I said.

Once they left, I headed downtown instead of my townhouse.

I'm a city girl. It was where the crazies were. It was where big buildings greeted homeless people next to business executives.

I parked in a parking garage so excited to start my new
journey. Where was Donny in all this? On my mind was
where he always remained, especially when I was manic.
I walked out of the garage on the way to nowhere in
particular. I was strolling around downtown San Antonio. It
was going to rain. The clouds were rumbling in, and it was
cold.
I walked to Denny's and ate. I had about $50 in my
wraparound purse.
The storm came in righteous, that's for sure. I was wearing
Bobo's old, grey, oversized sweatpants and they were heavy
with water.
I roamed along the Riverwalk running towards strangers to
join their conversations as they tried to get out of the rain
with their umbrellas. I didn't have an umbrella.
Some laughed and got a kick out of me. Some gave me a
frightened look and found a way out of my sight.
I ran up and down the stairs that led to the Riverwalk and
bars open for business on Christmas Day, but they would be
closing soon. It was still like a hurricane outside. I saw a bald
man in a kilt wearing combat boots at the doorway to a bar.
Rain didn't fall on him. He sat there like a statue with a
thumb pointing inside the pub.
I laughed and laughed as I headed around the corner
towards downstairs again, but I turned around because I felt
bad for laughing at him, but he was gone. Just like that,
vanished.
I went inside the bar and two men were in there, a customer
and a bartender. I plopped right next to the grey haired,
bucktoothed, customer. He reminded me of a cartoon.

"Did you see that guy just outside in a kilt?" I asked.

"I wish we could see what you see," he replied.

Did he really say that? That's what I heard.

"Can I have a drink?" I asked the bartender.

"Just one," he said. I paid for it and gave him a $5.00 tip even though I didn't have much money to go on.

"Need something to eat?" he asked as he pushed chips and salsa towards my drink. Before I took a bite, the customer said, "Can I have…" as he dipped a chip in my salsa, "some?". The bartender laughed at this guy's gall. I just stared at the bucktooth customer that I nicknamed Bugs as he wolfed down my snack.

"Where are you going?" he asked as he smacked my chips and salsa.

"I don't know," I said as I shrugged one shoulder.

"Don't look at me," the bartender said. "I'm married."

I was thinking, so? Why is he telling me this? I'm not interested.

"You can come with me to my hotel at the Grand Hyatt. I got a room there," Bugs said.

"OK," I said and downed my shot of Patron.

I thought he was trying to get me out of the rain. I told him I was lost and couldn't find my truck.

Bugs and I went up to his double-bedded hotel room and that was where I met his son for the first time.

I sat on the first bed, but then the freezing air from the hotel air conditioner made me shiver. I laid down in the bed covering myself up in my soaked sweatpants.

Bugs uncovered me and jerked off my drenched shoes, socks, and sweatpants. "Do your job," he said arrogantly.

I had no clue what he was talking about, but I felt dirty; did he think I was a prostitute?

All I had on was Bobo's tee shirt and my panties. I covered up as Bugs hung my sopping clothes in the shower.

Bugs and his son went down to the bar. I just sat there staring at the streetlights outside the window. Everyone knew who I was.

I got bored and put back on my soppy clothes. I went to the bar.

"One shot?" I asked the son.

"One," he said.

Last call was made.

"Jack and Diet Coke please," I ordered, and his son got the same.

"That's a hooker!" he said, and pointed in a black man's face who was wearing a wig and was bathed in cheap perfume.

I got angry.

"Why do people do that?" I asked.

"What?" he asked dumbfounded.

"What you just did! You pointed in that "woman's" face like she's not a person, but a sight to see on your trip? It's obvious, why make her feel bad?" I said, my face was red with anger.

He didn't know what to say.

Bugs joined us, "Man, I'd rather be doing work for my charity than being on this business trip," he said in slothfulness.

"You stole my chips and salsa!" I blurted out. I was known to hold on to grudges of people's character especially when in the middle of mania.

"You're FUBAR, woman!" he said. "Do you know what that means? Fucked up beyond all recognition!" he continued.

The bar closed.

The men went to their hotel room. I didn't want to go up there with them, so I sat down in the lobby staring at the TV. It was still storming outside with bursts of thunder.

"You can't stay here," an employee said as he approached me while I sat in the lobby.

"I have nowhere else to go," I said.

I guess it was like what Bobo used to say in the DJ booth, "You don't have to go home, but you can't stay here."

"But he stole my chips and salsa!" I exclaimed. I explained that Bugs took it. Like a schoolyard spat, the employee became a detective to find who had stolen Lara's chips and salsa.

The employee and I went to Bugs' floor.

Bugs opened the door to the employee who asked where my chips and salsa were.

"You ARE FUBAR!" Bugs said again and he handed me what little I left behind in the room.

I left the hotel with wind gusts knocking my balance off. I couldn't walk a straight line even if I was sober.

Everything was lit in Christmas lights, but I was the only one on the streets of downtown San Antonio to appreciate them.

I spent the night under a covered corner of a coffee shop.

Day came, sunny, pure, and blurry. My vision wasn't blurry, but my mind was foggy. I've been off my medications for days now.

I knew I parked my truck in a parking garage. I even wrote down the street it was on. Every time I passed that street, I could not see a parking garage. All afternoon, I searched for my truck. Then, I called my mom, with the little bit of juice I had left on my phone. I needed a ride from her.

When my mom arrived to meet me, we found it! Turned out, I circled it several times in my go-around. My mom paid the overnight fee. We separated to her reluctance.

The sun fell and night arrived. There were several clubs near my apartment. I put on my black hoodie and army pants with combat boots, only carrying my computer bag and purse. It was the only thing I had left in this world. Fuck my family. I'm going to a bar. It was pitch black, except for the streetlamps guiding my way. I wanted to walk instead of driving my truck, so people wouldn't follow me. I walked down the highway shoulder to get to Texas Gals, a strip club. Cops' lights flashed behind me.

One of the police officers came up to me. My first instinct was to run from him. However, I remembered it's illegal to not talk to cops when they come up to you. I learned that in Dallas the time I tried to ignore the police officer when I was doing nothing wrong. "Do you know it's illegal to walk down the highway?" the one said. "It is legal to walk down the access road."

"No," I didn't know.

"You can get hit and you're wearing black for God's sake! Where are you going?"

"To Texas Gals," I said.

I must be calm, was my silent mantra. That was another thing I learned by experience, or they would take me to the hospital. I still wasn't answering calls from my mom nor family members.

The officer asked the typical questions, "What's your name?"

I gave them my ID.

"Where are you going again?" he asked.

"Texas Gals. They are having a stripping contest tonight; I just want to sit and watch," I answered.

"You won't make it in time. It's 1:30 a.m. We'll take you there," the cop said like nothing was wrong as I was walking down the shoulder of a highway at night.

I sat in the back, without those tight as fuck handcuffs on me. They do that on purpose; that's another thing I learned on my travels.

Once at Texas Gals, the door girl asked for my ID.

"What do you want to drink?" she asked me.

I'd never been here before; every club I'd ever been to previously that had a waitress take your order then take your card.

I ordered a Rumple Minze on ice. More alcohol, more fun. Before they ran it through, I got my drink. I drank it.

A 6ft tall bouncer, about 300 pounds, came up to me about five minutes later.

"You got your free drink. Now it's time to leave. Your credit card didn't go through," he said firmly.

"That's y'all's fault," I snapped. "They didn't run my credit card before I ordered the drink. I'm not leaving by your hands. Call the cops."

I assumed the same nice cops would come and rescue me. The bouncer had no qualms calling the cops. More trouble for me I assumed he thought. Little did he know. These cops were genuinely nice and if anything, they would just take me to the hospital even though I didn't want to go. My mom had the police put in their system that I am disabled and bipolar so if I ever got arrested, they'd take me to the mental hospital instead of jail.

Sure enough, the same cops came. They asked to see my ID again.

"Do you know why you got kicked out?"

"My card was declined," I said cognizant.

"Your ID looks like a mugshot," he said.

It did. I took it when I was manic, smirking at the DMV picture taker, hating her attitude.

"Well, you're prohibited from coming here ever again. You can't even ever drive down this street. You're banned," he said just being a dick. I knew you couldn't be banned from an entire street.

I made my impression of what I thought the Virgin Mary would look like, all innocent.

"You seem okay with all this and you're not creating problems, so we'll take you home," the nice cop said. He put handcuffs on me this time, not tight though.

One cop talked about God all the way to my apartment.

God, shut up! I thought.

I laid down sideways in the car. Blah, blah, blah, I thought rolling my eyes.

They drove me home. I took a cat nap.

Morning came. Time for a walk. I did not take my truck again because I was paranoid that people knew my license plate number. They would follow me! I believed.

I walked miles and miles to Blockbuster with my purse and Blockbuster card.

I took off my hoodie and wrapped it around my waist. Today wasn't cold. In Texas, December weather was in the 70s and the sun was bright above me. The weather was like me, unpredictable.

I threw off my shirt. I was now just in my white sports bra and my dirty, mildew smelling sweatpants from my night a few days ago with Bugs.

I walked down the sidewalk swaying my hips fast, like speed walking.

When I got to Blockbuster, I stretched my leg up and kicked the door open with flare.

I was searching for the movie *Changeling*, a video I loved with Angelina Jolie as the star.

Within minutes, the cops came in arresting me. I was just searching through videos.

"What the fuck!" I screamed. "I didn't do anything!"

"We got a call that you were stealing," the tiny chick cop said.

"I wasn't stealing! I have a Blockbuster card! Check!" I screamed.

"Calm down ma'am or I'll have to arrest you," she said.

"How am I supposed to calm down? I don't steal!"

She grabbed my purse and searched through the crumpled-up trash.

She found it! My Blockbuster card. She tightly put on the handcuffs anyway because I wouldn't calm down.

"Those are tight as fuck! What is your problem? Oh, you must act big and bad to make your ego think you're in control?" I challenged her.

She shoved me in the car. After spending seconds in the cop car, I got claustrophobic, and my chest felt circular and like a black hole was rotating around in it. Everything was annoying and itched; it was hard to breathe. They took me to the hospital but didn't arrest me. I had done nothing wrong!

Following the latest breakup with Bobo, I was in the hospital every few months for two years.

Despite that hospitalization from the Blockbuster incident, I was still manic.

After two weeks of being drugged by cocktails of medication, I was discharged from the hospital.

I remembered my mom on the phone with me saying, "Lara, they always let you out of the hospital when you're still manic. You've become a good actress. You trick everyone but your family."

I didn't answer any phone calls for days. I didn't talk to my mom for weeks after this last hospital stay because she, to me, was the enemy. Every member of my close circle was my enemy. My newly found abusers were my true friends. They didn't medicate my mind to conform like everyone else.

The curtain closed.

Chapter 23

The curtain reopened.

In the next scene, I heard a knock on my door. I looked
through the peephole. It was the cops! I hadn't done
anything wrong, so I answered the door.
"Lara Murphy?" the cop asked.
"Yes," I answered without a shower in weeks. My cowlicks
and greasy hair exposed who I was.
"You're under arrest," he said with his partner standing by.
"For what? I am just sitting here in my apartment," I said,
voice high and cracking like someone angry and in puberty.
"We have a medical warrant on you," he said sternly.
I resisted. I wasn't calm at all. One carried me with my arms
and the other with my legs down the stairs.
I fought, legs and arms flailing with my head convulsing out
of control.
"At least find my keys and lock my door!" I screamed.
"We'll think about it," the mean one said.
Once out of the apartment and into the parking lot, the cops
and I fought. I flailed enough. I battled my way out of their
grasps, and I tried to kick the nice one in the balls. The other
one then pinned my head to the smoldering ground as the
sun heated it. It was like running down hot sand without
sandals at the beach, but instead of running, you had your
face pressed against it. I relented. It was so hot, it felt like a
burning stove.
One of the cops put handcuffs on me.

In the hospital again. These asshole cops talked and laughed about the fight and how I almost kicked the nice one in the balls as the nurse took my vitals.

The nurse admitted me, and the assholes left. I was worried about my apartment. They never locked it.

Later I found out my mom was the one who put the medical warrant on me. It was because I was not answering her calls and not opening the door when she knocked.

My mom packed what I had in a duffle bag. The cops gave her my keys. She locked my door and brought clean clothes to the hospital for me. That night, she also bought me new underwear, hoodies, and jogging pants. The nurse spread my panties all over the front counter as well as my hoodies and my pants. They had no discretion. They took my picture and made me take a shower. I also had to socialize, go to groups, and eat with them or I stay longer.

I called Bobo for the first time in months after our breakup. I called to ask for cigarettes.

"Hello?" he answered.

"Yo, Bobo."

"What, Lara?"

"I'm in the hospital in need of cigarettes," I said.

"I know you're in the hospital; your mom called and told me. When I go in town, I'll bring you some cigarettes," he said stoically.

"I need a lot of cigarettes. When can you come?" I asked impatiently.

"Like I said, when I'm in town. Maybe tomorrow or the next day," he said and hung up.

A few days later, the nurse called me up to the counter and said a man brought me a carton of cigarettes. I was not expecting a carton, that's for sure. The nurse wrote down my name on every pack.

"Here you go," I gave a pack to another patient.

"That's the nicest thing anyone has done for me in a long time," he said.

I went back to get myself a pack and saw a different nurse stealing them. I saw my name on the pack as she took it to the next room. Mistakenly, I thought she was my friend too, so I never told on her. I only got three packs out of those ten before the nurse stole the rest.

When it came time for visitors, my mom always came. One time, the nurse brought my dinner to me in the unit instead of the cafeteria. They gave my mom a dinner plate also so she and I could bond and eat together.

"They pissed in my tacos!" I exclaimed to my mom.

"I'm boring. I know," my mom said smiling when I looked at her. She meant she had nothing to talk about.

"I'm going to smoke with everyone else," I said as I saw others go out.

"Visit with your mom," one of the nurses said. "Visiting time will be over when you come back in."

"Bye, Mom," I said as I started heading outside.

The nurse pursed her lips and looked compassionately at my mom.

Out of anger learning she had placed a medical warrant out on me, I said, "I don't care if you never visit me again! In fact, I hope you don't!"

"Well, I won't buy you any more clothes then!" she said as her voice rose for the first time.

"You think you can buy my love with clothes?!" I said as other people visiting their loved ones gave snickers and sideways glances at me.

"Your Mom worked 10-to-11-hour days at a busy rehab hospital. She spent most of her days problem solving with families after their loved one suffered a stroke or brain injury. She prepared to find a home for them, helped them with insurance and emotional support, usually with impatient family members. Then every visit with you after her long day, your mom shops for you. Name brand clothes she buys, and you'd rather have a cigarette. You tell her you don't want to see her every day when she visits you, and yes, every day after work she's here and new clothes are a part of it." The voice inside the train said.

"She had the cops drag me out of my apartment just because I wasn't talking to her! I didn't ask her to buy me anything. I can wear the hospital scrubs for all I care!" I yelled back inside the train.

Cigarette breaks became so important to me I'd leave my family day after day if I had to. I just wanted to be around the people talking to themselves, rapping their own raps, or getting an employee to break the rules a little bit to let me see a YouTube video.

The curtain closed.

Chapter 24

The curtain reopened.

In the next memory, I was working again at Private Garden
after two weeks at this last hospital.
I was acting weird, the manager said. I was still manic.
Mitchell called my emergency contact, my mom. She told
him if he wanted me to leave, call the cops. My mom had
him call my sister too.
The management tried to get me dressed in the bathroom
but all they could get on me was my jacket over my stripping
clothes. The cops came into the restroom to get me, and I
carried my purse with a dead cell phone battery and $10. I
left the rest of my civilian clothes in the restroom.
Darcy arrived with her husband and talked the cops into
letting her drive my truck to the local grocery store where
she'd leave it! The cops gave my keys to my sister without
question. She took off as her husband drove their SUV. That
made no sense! Why take my truck in the first place?
The cops left. Everyone thought everything was taken care
of, but they didn't realize I had no phone and only had $10. I
was wearing a see though white slip with black knee-high
stiletto boots and a jacket that barely hit my waist. It was
after midnight, and I was stranded. I walked down the street
looking like a hooker. I couldn't walk safely like this! I lived
close to the club, but the keys to my apartment were on the
keychain my sister took. Even if I managed to get to my
apartment, how could I get in?

A car stopped right away with two young men inside and the driver asked me if I needed a ride. I took it. These men took me to where the cops said my sister would leave my truck. Darcy and her husband were waiting there praying and crying. Oh please! Save it. I thought. I could have died and now I got to my truck anyway.

"We just didn't know what to do," was my sisters' answer. "I was afraid if you got into our SUV for a ride that you'd punch me, or even kill me!" she said sobbing.

None of this "logic" made sense to me, even as a "crazy" person. I drove off.

The curtain closed.

Chapter 25

The curtain reopened.

A week later I drove to my sister's house – still manic but maybe no one would notice. I drove there to have some quality time with the little ones, my nieces and nephew.
Darcy told me beforehand it was ok to spend time with the kids. She said she'd make lunch for everyone.
Darcy answered the door.
"Com'on in sis, lunch is almost ready," she said.
We all sat at the kitchen table and had time to chat before I would shove my face with yummy food my sister would make.
I couldn't help it. My mania always finds an opportunity to cause unrest.
"Do you know God is the biggest terrorist?" I asked Darcy.
The kid's eyes spun around to meet mine. Innocent ears were mine to greet. They were so used to praising God and asking for forgiveness and you'll go to Heaven.
"Lara," Darcy said and gave a stern look with pursed lips noticing the kids noticing me.

"I mean, you have to do what He says or else you'll burn in Hell for eternity!?" I continued. "And then what about you, Darcy? We are taught to love each other because we are family, right? What would happen when you go to Heaven, and I go to Hell? You would be in so much bliss, it would be like you never knew me. While you're in Heaven you would never think of me again while I rot in Hell forever. Does that show compassion?" I asked. "You would be like 'oh, my sister is in Hell, oh well, fuck her, she chose free will and didn't ask for forgiveness and now I'm in Heaven' and then you'd sing a Christmas carol Fa la la la la, la la la la," I sung for her.

"Grab her keys!" my sister screamed to her husband.

It took me awhile to realize what Darcy was talking about. Then I understood she was going to trap me again without a ride for simply having an opinion.

"You always speak of the Devil when you're manic, Lara!" she screamed, ordering the kids to their rooms.

Her husband snatched my keys off the table.

"I was just going to leave, Darcy! Give me my keys and I'll be gone!" I screamed back. "You're doing this because I questioned God! Really?"

"I'll call the cops," she threatened.

I regretted the kids seeing this, but damn, my sister was out of her flipping mind! Doesn't she remember a week ago when her and her husband stole my property (my car keys) and left me stranded?

The adults went outside. And I was pissed. Being "crazy" was ok; being crazy and having an opinion, not so much.

I pulled my sister's long hair until her husband put me in a headlock as they waited for the cops to come.

The cops pulled up and after ten minutes I got my keys back and drove off. Typically, I am nice and don't share my opinion where it doesn't belong. But mania is my escape and I relish the freedom of not giving a fuck. When I go outside this "good girl" spell though, people can't handle it.

The curtain closed.

Chapter 26

The curtain reopened.

Although I hid my psychosis, I was back in the hospital after a month. All my acting was caught. I never admitted myself into the hospital. The cops or my persistent mom always took me to the holding cell (the freezing waiting room) of the hospital. With my mom's observations and accusations, these nurses only listened to her testimony. I am the patient, not her, and that pissed me off. I was right there in the room with my mom and the nurses never looked at me. I wasn't a person.

Finally, my mom left, and I waited for hours for the nurses to finish up paperwork. These employees had heated rooms behind a plexiglass window and observed me much like a think tank.

I stared blankly at the regular TV program. Suddenly, static sizzled across the television and a dark-haired seemingly news woman with glassy eyes said, "There are aliens here disguised as human beings!" Immediately after that, static turned the TV grey and black again and a blonde-haired woman finished her news report; the blonde said nothing about aliens. No one else in the waiting room seemed to have seen this television special. It was directed only for me to see.

That's it! I am in a spaceship, I thought and rolled everywhere around the holding cell in my chair on wheels. A pasty, bald nurse grew impatient and demanded me to stop or he would stop me.

I rolled around hastily against the nurse's disapproval. He jerked out of his chair and out of the "think tank". Then he rushed me into a dark room where I only saw shadows of him and the female nurse. He hoisted me on the gurney as I fought back. I fell on the ground.

The imbecile then yanked my hair and ripped it when he tried to get me on the table. Regardless, I kept all my weight on the ground. I looked at the other nurse and she looked scared because she heard my hair rip also. Nothing seemed to work for this asshole, so he put his hands around my waist and threw me on the table again. This time the other nurse helped control my spastic arms.

The jerk then pulled down my pants and panties; right before he stuck the needle into my butt cheek, his eyes flipped to the back of his head and glowed neon white in the pitch-black room. I was positive he was an alien.

After he injected me, that was it. I did not remember anything else.

The curtain closed.

Chapter 27

The curtain reopened.

The conductor sped up the train. On the subway platform, it looked like he fast forwarded two years of episodes from a TV remote. The conductor then slowed down for one scene that he made sure I would never forget.
From fast forward to play, the lights were on the stage in front of me.
Through the plexiglass I saw myself as I chipped paint off a shed. My friend, whom I helped with this work let me stay there as I requested. He had to momentarily go take care of another project.
It was lunch time, and the owner of the shed was home. I played loud country music. The owner came out of her house twice to politely ask me to turn it down. After the second time she came out, I grabbed my purse and called it a day.
I walked to my apartment close by. I dumped out my messy purse to find my keys. My keys were missing! I knew I put them in there, so I wondered why I didn't find them. This always happened when manic; I would lose things and it was as if the sky gulped them up.
Frustrated, I walked to the office of the apartment complex and requested a new key. The lady at the desk told me to come back later and she would give me a new one with a $50 fee. To kill some time, I walked to the local grocery store to get a quick bite for lunch.

Everyone saw me. Everyone laughed at me. Everyone gave me dirty looks. So, I started to leave without lunch. I didn't know why, but I grabbed my crotch over my jeans and snorted like a pig. I then flipped off the security camera and walked out.

Imaginary rain clouds seemed to drizzle out split pea soup until the entire air I walked through was gooey, humid, and green. It wasn't raining, but my manic perception overruled logic.

Without an apartment key, I strolled around the neighborhood.

Some construction workers fixing a roof looked at me as I glared at them. "La puta," one of them yelled at me.

Even the guy mowing his lawn with a black pillowcase over his face – executioner style - turned to look in my direction.

Any self-worth I ever had was gone. It was as if I didn't have eyes of my own anymore; I had everyone else's eyes directed inward to my psyche.

I found my way back to my apartment. I knocked on my neighbor's door. He answered the door. "Can I come in?" I asked apologetically. We always got along so he let me in.

"Please, please! I need to know I am real! I am fading!" I cried.

"Calm down. What's wrong?" he asked.

"Do you have a gun?"

"No! No!" he yelled. "What's going on?" he continued.

"Please! I need to kill myself!" in desperation I pleaded.

"Is there someone I can call for you?" he asked.

I stripped naked. "Here, take me! Fuck me!" I insisted.

"I don't know what is going on with you, but you have to put your clothes back on," the 50 something man said.

"Everyone hates me!" I kept on.

"How about your mom's number, do you know that?" He tried to calm me down.

The emotional pain was so bad that, for once, I did not mind if my mom took me to the hospital.

"Yes!" I said and gave him the digits.

The neighbor talked to her as I paced frantically around his living room. I got dressed. My mom left work and was at my neighbor's place in 15 minutes.

In her car, she listened to a program with someone preaching about the Bible. On the way to the hospital, I tried to unhear what was being preached.

We got to the hospital. "I want to walk myself in with my boots on," I told my mom as she parked just outside the admissions office. I started walking the opposite way because I was confused about where to go.

"Lara! Lara!" My mom stepped out of her car and yelled.

I started sprinting. She ran after me in her work heels and pencil skirt. My mom screamed my name the whole time and found a nurse who also ran after me. They caught up to me when I stopped and talked to some patients who were smoking cigarettes. I didn't know why these patients were outside, but, oh well, they were my kind of people. Immediately, the personnel were not worried about admitting me; instead, they took me straight to the clinic. My mom, against all procedure, was in the hallway with me. Irritated by my mom's presence I pushed past the nurses.

"I don't want to be here!" I wailed.

Out of survival, I ran down a hall in the men's unit and everyone including my mom ran after me. There was a glass door, and I was going to escape.

"It's locked!" one nurse shrilled.

I ran into the door then crumpled to the ground. My lip gushed full of blood. My teeth went straight through my lip. I thought I lost my teeth, at least one tooth, but thankfully I didn't.

The nurses put me out with a shot. I woke up with stitches and a crooked smile.

Lights out.

The curtain closed.

Chapter 28

The curtain reopened.

I got a new phone number and had blocked Bobo from my Facebook account during the two years of mania. Bobo called my mom once a month to see how I was doing. I walked around the park one day when most of my mania subsided and I wondered what if Bobo died and I heard nothing about it. I called and he picked up.
"Hello," he answered.
"Hi," I said.
He was silent.
Then we talked for about an hour, and he agreed to see me.
"Lara, let's just see where this goes," he said hesitantly.
For months we talked. I wanted a third chance.
"It'll be different," I said.
"That's what you told me the last two times," he professed.
He gave me another chance anyway.
The curtain closed.

Chapter 29

Bobo was a pot head.

The entire time we've known each other, he never knew I disliked weed. I smoked because I felt it was his lifestyle and I wanted to fit in. He told me marijuana makes people relax. Bobo joked that I could get a medical marijuana license because I am "certifiable". He meant I was mental, and they should give it to those in need.

Instead of chilling, weed affected me differently. It made me uncomfortable and crazier. It was like my thoughts swirled around my head and popped out of my eyeballs. It was like everyone, more than before, was staring at me and could read my mind. Weed made me more anxious, not less.

Chapter 30

The curtain reopened.

In this scene, outside on the platform again, I saw myself hugging Bobo around his waist waiting in the concession stand line at the movies. I was surprised he didn't care what other people thought about the crazy lady attached to him, scared of the public. He held my hand when he paid for our hotdogs, candy, drinks, and popcorn.
I only took my head off his chest when he handed me my soda. In the theatre people slumped in their seats and I heard them snoring before the movie began. Automatically, I knew this was because of me. These people pretending to be asleep were all spies. They were loud. It was not like one person was snoring; it was like a symphony of snores. They were trying to tell me that I was so boring that I needed to change or die because I wasn't born here to be fake. I was a nervous wreck and basically a mouse agreeing with everyone, without voicing my own opinion. They all woke up for the movie, but Bobo fell asleep holding my hand the entire movie. That was sweet. That night, we went back to my apartment and had sex. I will never forget this time because at the finish, he tasted like the best mixture of cherry and strawberry cotton candy topped off with Werther's Original caramel candy all up in my mouth. Mania makes everything taste magical and no one else could even fathom how true that was.
The curtain closed.

Chapter 31

I didn't live with Bobo yet, but we were dating.
Just after that wonderful memory, a nightmare began in the
train I was riding.
Steel plates slid themselves across the plexiglass windows of
the train and bolted shut. My voices spoke, *"You may not
remember this, but we do. Let me remind you today of that
which you did not remember nor will remember for the rest
of this journey."*
Then, as if my third eye acted like a film projector the vision
plastered itself onto the steel plates like a movie. *"Lights
off,"* the voices commanded, and the conductor turned
them off.

Chapter 32

I wandered for what seemed like several miles at night down a deserted road. My pajama bottoms were straggling through the dirt and mud. I stuck out my thumb at the stray cars that passed by. Finally, a truck stopped. He rolled down the window.

"Wait here if you want a ride, I'll be back. If you move, I'll find you," he said.

I did not like that, but paralyzed out of fear, I didn't see a better option. I had no clue where I was, I had no clue where I was going. This guy was the only person that offered me a way out. Mania didn't care that I might be getting back with Bobo. Mania made me fly from one subject to the next because it's the disease. Sometimes you just gotta go. And this night I had to go, but I roamed without a destination.

I waited next to the endless, dying trees to my left and to my right. Then, the man who offered me a ride roughly ten minutes ago found me and he had five other guys with him. A cute guy in the cab of the black diesel truck rolled down the automatic window. He had long, shiny, black hair and he was skinny with a big welcoming smile. I smiled back. Meanwhile, in the front of the cab, as if in slow motion, a scary, big, bald white man with welts all over his stone-cold face offered me a pill. He said if I didn't take it, they would all rape and kill me in the woods.

Nothing could phase me in mania. No amount of alcohol could even give me a buzz. "Watch and see, this drug won't affect me in any way," I said. So, I took the pill. They laughed. The good looking one said, "By the time you get in the truck, you won't know where you are nor how you got here."

"Where am I?" I thought as I sat on the lap of one of the five men. They ranged in age from 25 to 45 years old.

"Do you know how you got in this truck?" one of them asked.

"No," I replied. It was like being in a dream state. I didn't know if it was a dream, but it was scary.

"See I told you! *This* drug will phase you," they all laughed.

"It's the date rape drug," he said.

To me, none of this was real. It was like making a horrible mistake that I wished I would wake up from.

"Where's your house?" one of them asked.

"I don't know," I said.

"If you can't find your house, we'll go back to the woods we found you in and kill you!" he said.

I was terrified and searched my memory. I looked around and saw a familiar street.

"There!" I exclaimed. "That street!"

"That was just down the street," the driver said.

I thought I was further than I was because mania distorts time. It was down a road I never went down before even though it was close to home.

Once at my apartment, we piled in. I let them in because it was five against one and they threatened to kill me if I didn't. If I said "no" or screamed rejecting what they wanted, I knew they'd beat me or leave me for dead. They wanted me to take a shower and shave, so, I did. While I shaved, one of them took a dump, it smelt like dog shit, and it clogged up my toilet. Before leaving the bathroom, he peeked in on me in the shower.

Outside the shower they wanted me to put on makeup, to "look pretty for them."

After that, everything got distorted. I could remember some things, but the date rape drug left most things fuzzy for me. When my makeup was done, one of them asked if I wanted to snort a line of cocaine. I agreed. I was naked because I just got out of the shower. I snorted half a line when he shoved his massive dick into my ass. That's when it began. He raped me from behind forcing me to my knees. He told me to snort like a pig, then moo like a cow. He came in my vagina after fucking my ass.

 Next, another one of them shoved my mouth down on his dick till I couldn't breathe. "Swallow it bitch!" Soon after he finished in my mouth, the rest of the animals had their turns. They saved the guy with the welts all over his face for last. He told me he had AIDS.

The whole time my intuition knew I had to comply to these rapists' demands or things would get worse for me.

"Anyone got a condom?" he asked the rest of the defilers. They paused.

"Are you sure, man?" one asked. "Why?"

"Because she's nice," the AIDS guy said.

"I'll give you ten seconds before I change my mind," the man with AIDS said.

The others fumbled through their wallets. One gave the AIDS guy a condom, and all five were quiet.

AIDS man put on the condom and fucked me. Finally, they were all done. The next thing I remember was being naked holding my legs tight to my chest as they tried to get to know me. The guy with AIDS asked for my name and social security number so he could find me if I moved. I gave it to him out of fear.

Chapter 33

A few hours later, I woke up because someone was banging on my door, like the cops do when someone is in trouble, and they want to get their attention. I looked down at my naked body. There were bruises everywhere but my face. Nothing hurt though.

I had moisture everywhere! It was running out of my ass and vagina, plus I had an awful taste in my mouth! I threw on a robe. It was the AIDS guy at the door. I remembered him; the date rape drug hadn't worn off yet. I opened my door scared about what he would do.

"I wanna feel it. I wanna get mine," he said. He came in and locked both locks behind himself. "You must have some hair gel, right? All girls have hair gel. Make your hair messy," he said. I did and after I walked out of the bathroom, he proceeded to shove my face down on the carpet and lifted my robe. He must have liked a distressed victim with him wanting my hair a mess and all. The scariest part was when he unbuckled his belt. The clink was so forceful and so loud, as if on purpose.

He wanted to know who this would impact. "There must be someone you fuck," he said. "There's gotta be someone," he claimed.

"What's his name?"

"Bobo," I said, with tears streaming down my face.

"There we go," he said softly as he pumped, like pumping for oil. He hit gold; his name was Bobo.

It wasn't just rape. He wanted to get to the core of me. He wanted to make me cry and be in agony. That's why he had me mess up my hair. He wanted me to hurt the person I cared for, Bobo.

"And, he won't even know you have AIDS," he said. "You'll give it to him. Ahh," he sighed, and he was done and gone.

"Do I Have AIDS?!" I asked the voice.

"No, you're lucky. Remember you got tested several times later. All the time, because you're paranoid. The tests are always negative. Not everyone exposed to AIDS gets AIDS on the first time," the voice said.

The voices showed compassion this time because they weren't altogether harmful. At times like these, they were my friends. It was not like they hated me. They were just hard on me trying to teach me how to feel again, to feel love, to feel something, anything. This I knew to be true. I loved my voices no matter what because they made me feel special. Not everyone has pals in their mind like me.

My uncle came by the morning after the gang rape to make sure I took my meds. He did this every morning. My uncle arrived several hours after the date rape drug wore off.

I didn't remember a thing about the night before. I threw on my dirty pajamas that I wore when I wandered down the street the night before. He said my eyes were rolling back, my mascara streamed down my face, my hair was messed up and I was shaking.

He took me to the hospital.

Back in the train, the lights came back on, and the metal plates slid back in place. The showcase of this past event was over. I couldn't remember why the lights turned off in the first place. I couldn't remember anything. My voices showed me the rape, but since I was on a date rape pill when it happened, it was still hard to remember anything from that time. Even though it projected through me onto the steel slates of the train. I was unconscious through the whole showing of the rape.
The curtain closed.

Chapter 34

The curtain reopened.

While I was in the hospital, Bobo and I continued to see each other.
Because of all my past hospitalizations, I had to go before a judge when I was released. If I didn't take my medication, he threatened to put me in a governmental institution for the rest of my life. The judge did not realize where all these manic episodes came from.
"I do take my meds, but when the TV or radio gives me subliminal messages, I turn manic. I don't know what day or night is when that happens. Time runs together and because of this, I forget to take my meds!" I exclaimed.
"I don't believe you," the all-knowing king said. "What do these subliminal messages say?" he asked.
I started smirking. "I will never tell you", I said. "It's a secret and none of your business," I concluded. "Private things are private," I hushed.
The curtain closed.

Chapter 35

The curtain reopened.

I moved in with Bobo for the third time.
"This time will be different!" I reassured him.
"That's what you said the last time, too," he said helping me
pack my stuff in his truck.
It lasted for a month until I went manic again. During our
time together Bobo and I made up songs for each other,
danced around the house, and he taught me how to bow
hunt. We also dove hunted.
I remember once I tried to make him dinner when he got
home from work. I thought I followed the directions of
heated-up meals, but he could barely eat it. He kissed me
anyway before going to his second job: wild game trap and
transport. That's where he basically hung out of a helicopter
trying to dart exotic animals to send to a ranch somewhere.
I gulped all my pills at night with water, unlike
recommended. Bobo kept warning me not to do that
because it was not what the doctor said. I did not think
anything of it. But here it came, total insanity. I felt it.
Bobo asked me to marry him for the third time. Every time I
moved in with him, a proposal was asked. I said yes, but my
arm still throbbed for Donny. I found Donny on Facebook,
and it was just a matter of time. It was a device I couldn't
itch out. I needed closure before marriage. I never stopped
being manic, just happy-go-lucky and thinking all was well
with me when I wasn't well in my brain.

The next day Bobo and I went to the Private Garden for him to visit some of our friends at the club. Afterwards, he started walking down the street. I followed him. He saw a pawn shop and asked me to wait outside. I knew he was going to buy me a ring and it scared me. I didn't think I was ready.

That same night Bobo wanted to take me out. His plans involved us going to a carnival in this small town of Ingram, Texas.

"I don't want to go," I said.

"Lara, we don't do anything but watch TV; Will you go for us?" he asked.

"Okay," was my reply.

"Alright then," he said happily. Bobo said he was good at carnival games and that he would win me the biggest stuffed animal so everyone would be jealous, like he did for his daughters.

I smiled.

Once at the carnival, I switched moods when I saw a woman in line for tickets ahead of us. The back of her shirt said, *I love NYC.* It triggered me to think about Donny and when we lived in New York City. My arm began to throb. It was a message from Donny. I knew I would visit Donny once Bobo returned to his primary job at the oil rig. He was leaving soon.

Bobo and I went to several token booths to see if he could win me a prize. He was slightly off that day so there was no luck getting a stuffed animal.

There was a country band playing live. I didn't know how good Bobo could dance. Other than when he was being romantic dancing with me in the kitchen while preparing food, we didn't really dance. I was happy and surprised; this man had rhythm! Shouldn't I have known this before? Offset from having fun with Bobo that night, was this bright red burn in my forearm throbbing and it was hard to ignore.

"Let's sit down, this purse is bothering me," I said.

"I'll hold it," he said.

Many women would have loved a man who could dance, and play guitar, be a great lover and sweetheart like Bobo with all his other good qualities. But I was embarrassed of a man holding my purse!

"No, I want to leave!"

I completely turned into a bitch. He wanted to stay but I just wanted to get in touch with Donny.

"Did I do something wrong?" he asked. I knew he would never dance with me again and I'd regret my actions and thoughts.

At home I sat on the couch on one side of the sectional. I told him, "I'm not ready to get married".

"Thanks for telling me," Bobo said, stoic, as he sat on the other end of the couch. "I'm not happy," I said. I wasn't happy, but not because of him. The next two or three nights I ran out of my antipsychotics. As we lay down together, I heard him crying but I didn't care. I gave him the cold shoulder when he tried to reach out for what we once held just a short month ago. Mania caught up to me rapidly and I went from love to hate quickly.

The curtain closed.

Chapter 36

The curtain reopened on the platform outside of the subway.

Bobo asked me what I wanted to eat a few days before he had to go back to the rig. I wanted his special spaghetti that took about an hour to make.
"He slaved over the stove making Greek pasta. He did this for you!" the voice/commentator spoke.
While waiting for the food, I turned on MTV and listened to everyone; I thought they were talking about me and joking with me. I sat on the edge of the coffee table listening intently to the TV. The TV got all my giddiness and flirtatious attention. Bobo asked me to get off his table several times. Next thing I knew, he pushed me off.
I started calling him every name in the book to hurt him. I lashed out. I was full-blown manic. I ran out of my antipsychotics days ago, so I was on edge.
"You're a pussy, Bobo!" I screamed. "People just use you. You're ugly! And have a big nose," I concluded.
If I felt any remorse for my scathing words, it was when I told Bobo that he had a big nose because that was said to me a few times growing up. I knew how much it hurt for someone to say that to me; now I had done it to Bobo!
I immediately said I was sorry, and I didn't mean it. I felt his wounds inside my heart at that moment. I learned you cannot take back those words.

The spaghetti was ready; he brought me a plate then served himself. I stood. I threw the plate of spaghetti all over him like a saucer as he waved it off. It splattered the ceiling, him, and the gold covered interwoven couch.

I went up to Bobo and bit his hand as hard as I could.

He stood up and pushed me. It was just a little tap from him, but it knocked me off my feet. I began biting his hand while on the ground and he jerked me towards the ground again. I got up, ran into his room to search for his gun. He always kept it by the bed. Always. It wasn't there. "Your gun's not there!" Stone cold without feeling, I was going to kill him. This feeling of cold and rage in the center of my being consumed me. I was a snake. How dare he push me! I will show him. My empathy for what I told him left me the second he decided to push me off the table.

I ran into the living room, held my hands out like a gun and shot him right between the eyes with my fingers. "You're dead," I said. They were there in the room. The shadows in each corner. My demons.

As if nothing happened, I asked if we could play chess after a while of silence. I wanted him to see I was smarter than him. He was calm and tried to calm me down. We never played chess before. I attacked the board with no plan. He easily won three times in a row.

I then took off my clothes, got on the couch and spread my legs while playing with myself.

"You know you want this. How does it feel to be used? I used every part of you," I said creepily. I did that to put a dagger through his heart. I never used him.

He somehow managed to lock me in his room from the outside. How he did that was magic to me. I tried hard to fight it.

At that point, I screamed in frustration and decided to sneak out the bedroom window still naked. He lived in a house by the river and houses were far apart.

I screamed lies for Bobo to hear through the door to hurt him.

"Oh yeah Bobo, how does it feel for someone to use you? You worthless piece of shit!" I screamed. Nothing was happening, so I knocked on the front door. He let me in. To keep me from going outside again, he hog tied me like the game animals at work with anything he could find - ties, ropes, whatever. I submitted because it was terribly uncomfortable. Then I cursed him some more. This whole occurrence happened over again about three times. I was still naked with arms and legs tied back, my back arching. Finally, he got me back in his room and once again secured the door from the outside. I was impressed, but I couldn't let him know that.

Ugly words flew out of my mouth again. Bobo barged in and pinned me down on the bed, covering my mouth; it was all he could take. I bit his hand again. He never said a bad word about me during all this. I let go. I didn't want to fight anymore, I just wanted to see Donny.

I don't know how, but I fell asleep that night. I slept peacefully. I awoke in the morning and planned on getting a plane ticket to New York City to see Donny. I would get a plane ticket as soon as Bobo went back to his other job as a driller on an oil rig.

As soon as he left, I began redecorating his house so to speak. I put rose quartz in the corners of the room to create magic and love for Donny and me. I constantly checked to see if Donny was on Facebook. He never was.

I threw away the picture of Bobo's first bow hunt where he caught a big deer. I also threw away my favorite outfit of his. He looked too good in it. I just wrecked the place. Then, I cut off all my hair and left it on the counter for him to find. And finally, I drank all his hard-to-find moonshine that his distant friend made for him years ago and I didn't feel a thing.

I acted like nothing was wrong when Bobo called. He apologized, and like what my family had told me, he said he didn't know what to do. I was uncontrollable. The last thing Bobo said to me on the phone was, I love you. He did nothing wrong. I had tried to kill him! And I did emotionally. After that conversation I ignored all his phone calls. I was determined to find out what all this arm throbbing thing was about Donny.

Bobo called my mom and told her I was going manic. He didn't mention anything else. Bobo had no contact with me because I rejected all of his calls. Just a month ago we were having fun together with me moving back in. But as soon as I ran out of antipsychotics, all I wanted was Donny- my old NYC flame that I met in acting class.

I bought a plane ticket and only took my computer, uncharged phone, and purse with no money in it. And one more thing - I brought the rose quartz that Donny gave to me at the end of our relationship. I planned to live and stay in New York City with Donny. I wanted him to be surprised that I kept that stone for so long.
The curtain closed.

Chapter 37

"How do you feel now, Lara? Now that there is no going back? No more music together, and no more love? Did you even love? Did you really love him? You may never know that though. You chose to take this journey of your own accord. Now, where are you going?"

In the train, I stood still and did not feel a beat anywhere in my heart. What heart?

I hated my whole family, even Bobo and my friends. I could not feel love. It would be fine to never see any of them again. I wanted the freedom my delusions and illusions gave me when manic. I would see things others couldn't. I've seen it! And everyone thinks I'm crazy.

The curtain reopened.

This whole ride was chaos. On the platform edge of the subway, I saw Bobo and the past, and yet, inside the train, my arm began throbbing again. It was Donny and my memory of him, of our brief six-month romance circulating through my heart and mind.

When Donny asked me to marry him, I was silent. I knew it was impossible back then. I wasn't ready. I didn't even know if I wanted to. This arm thing kept itching. What did he want to tell me? Snippets of memories with Donny entered my mind. Like the sarong he wore in the morning as he talked on the phone with a lit cigarette.

Outside the train I saw Bobo again, although Donny was on my mind. My neurotic brain circled around subjects, **racing.**

It was September 11, 2011, a decade since the 9/11 attacks when the Twin Towers were hit by terrorists. I was on a plane to what I thought was NYC with my hair cut to the scalp. I had left my hair on the kitchen counter for Bobo to find as the last piece of me he could ever have.

A man whose seat was next to mine on the plane immediately said to the flight attendant that he'd wait for the next plane; then he turned around and left the aircraft. I must have scared him. All was good because I got his window seat.

Most of the plane ride I laughed. I laughed because I couldn't contain it. The passengers exchanged frightened looks at me. They must have thought I was a threat.

Getting out of the plane was a real surprise.

"I'm in New Jersey, not New York City!"

It was 9 p.m. There was one last bus. I rushed to catch it out of the airport. I had no money. The only things I carried of true importance were my computer and the rose quartz Donny gave me when we dated.

There was the bus.

It came right when I got to the bus stop.

There were mostly ethnic people getting on this bus. A nicely dressed lady told me to be careful, it was a bad neighborhood. I was a bald woman, wearing combat boots and army pants. I hoped no one thought I was a white supremacist by the way I dressed.

"Oh, I don't have any money," I said to the bus driver.

The bus driver said it was okay. He waved me through with kindness in his eyes.

I stood out like the singer Bjork as a carbon copy.

"Last stop," the bus driver said.

"Last stop?" I asked.

I was still in New Jersey! Donny's office was in New York! The bus driver, who didn't seem to look at anyone leaving, looked at me with kindness. I looked at him, scared. I was the last one to leave the bus.

My voices assured me that Donny was on his way to ask me again to marry him. I forgot all about everyone in Texas, including Bobo, my fiancé.

I sat and waited all night on the streets- cold, hungry, and hugged my legs as I leaned against a brick wall. My voices kept me company.

While I was sitting on the chilly New Jersey concrete, my voices said, *"We're making great music up here!"* I looked up to the top floor of the abandoned brick building in front of me and thought, that's where the rock gods are playing music about me.

A cab came by the curb I was sitting on. I saw holograms of rock stars coming out of the taxi in front of me. Different images of separate bands of rock reached the doorstep beside me and the last one was Marilyn Manson. My voices said, *"She'd do everyone! Even Marilyn Manson!"* They had no reason for saying that.

Morning came. Totally manipulative, my voices told me to touch myself, you know, down there. They said if I did, Donny would come pronto. *"Show him how much you care,"* they said.

I started and hesitated; it didn't feel right. As soon as I reached my privates over my pants, a car followed by a swarm of more cars swirled around me. They drove back and forth, as the drivers stared at me with glassy eyes. Instantly, I got up. The sky became green again. I was scared for the first time by my schizoid mind. I dropped to my knees as people packed the sidewalks along the stores. I was in the middle of the sidewalk. People swerved around me like ants as if someone stepped in an ant pile. I prayed. No one cared. Maybe they thought I was on drugs or homeless. I was invisible to them. I didn't care.

I prayed, and then like The Matrix, no one was on the sidewalks anymore. I looked up into a department store window and prayed to a mannequin as if it was Donny. Still on my knees, and still with no one around, it was just me and the mannequin. I prayed hard saying I was sorry. I didn't want to stay in place to wait for him. The mannequin just stared at me blankly.

Feeling rejected, I left the rose quartz Donny gave me on a nearby bench. Maybe someone would find it who needs it. I closed my eyes and for some odd reason pictured a gynecologist tool used to go up your vagina during checkups and shoved the imaginary speculum up in the air. My voices laughed. Then I saw a bright, stunning white light going from the base of my pelvis to the center of my chest. Then another light from the crown of my head to meet at the center of my chest as well.

There the pulsing started. The filthy, ugly, pulsing, plunger feeling of this intense orgasm. People reappeared on the streets, trickling down into swarms. I walked as fast as I could with this pulsing. One guy looked at me and said, "Dumb," as loud as his mind could shout.

I looked for a way to die. An opportunity appeared to the right.

I saw the entrance to the subway. No attendant!

"Why?" I wondered. "Who cares why!" I dashed into the subway's shadows.

I sat on the platform bench, tightening my legs as much as I could.

My ride on this train was about to end. I had come full circle.

"I know you like this. Tighten your legs as much as you can, it won't stop, bitch. You love yourself too much to kill yourself. Too vain," my voices chimed in.

Here it comes!

Hop, skip, jump, that's all I need to do. It will be simple and easily over.

After the first train went past, I was on the edge awaiting the second one.

"We'll leave you alive but physically disabled! If you jump!" the voices said.

While in the train, I saw visions, horrible visions of me and what I'd done. It was a recap so I could never forget.

Through the plexiglass I saw images. Images of me hitting my mom and throwing hot coffee on her face. "Whore! Ugly piece of shit!" I'd scream at her at the hospital.

Then, in the train, I saw a memory of myself jumping out of my mom's car and running down the highway.

I saw her bring candy to all the patients. The patients smiled towards my mom.

"She's a bitch!" I brainwashed them. Then, she'd come in and they'd give her dirty looks.

She slumped in the visitor's chair every day, but she would show up. I'd have a cigarette break instead of visiting with her. Nurses would show disappointment on their faces.

In the train, I had visions of my mom in the hospital. Day after day she would check in with brand nice new clothes for me at the desk. She had style.

I also had memories of Bobo and all I had said to him.

"You're ugly. You're a pussy," I once said.

I saw him sitting there slumped back in the chair taking it.

I saw us playing chess.

I saw him cooking me pasta and I saw me throwing it at his face.

Worst of all, I saw me try to kill Bobo and I did mentally.

From the beginning of all this, I never stopped violently shaking my head in the train.

I couldn't take it.

The train sped up and I went flying to the back of the car, hitting my head on a pole in the subway.

"You got on this train now you've reached your destination. Here is your Road to Hell. Get out of this train, trash," a voice from inside the train sneered.

Chapter 38

Suddenly, I was outside the train, once again having this expanding orgasm. I didn't walk outside the train; it was just like this trip down memory lane never happened.

"Was it all a dream? Am I real? Is this real? What's real? I'm dying!" This train ride left me confused.

Once outside the train, the terminal was packed!

"Where did all these people come from?" I questioned.

There was an attendant watching all that was happening now.

"What is this? All these people? An attendant now? There wasn't an attendant when I jumped over the rails the first time. That was how I was able to be here because I had no metro card nor money," I asked my voices, they were silent. Cops and EMT's were surrounding the train. No one looked at me as I ducked under the caution tape. The song *Living Dead Girl,* by Rob Zombie echoed as I ran past and ran through people like a ghost. I didn't care to try to make sense of it. I thought it was just my mania making me invisible. I wanted to get out of there.

I ran, ran, ran up the steps and away from the truth, but what was the truth? Was I hallucinating or was this real? I was convinced that what I hallucinated was the ultimate truth, only private eyes would see.

Street signs lapped into one another. I thought I was walking in circles.

As I walked, desperate for the first time on this sidewalk to be safe, I was scared. I wanted to call my mom. My phone was dead.

I walked nowhere. There were run-down shops and dilapidated houses. I could've easily been a target.

I heard a man in an automobile shop say, "I'll pay ten dollars". I thought he was talking about me, like a whore. The orgasm kept going. It seemed like forever. I was in trouble now. I saw a park and it was the start of a cold night. I didn't have a jacket and I sat at the back of a tall tree. I closed my eyes tight, so tight they hurt. I'm going to get raped, maybe killed, I worried. I had nowhere to go. I am spending the night here, I thought.

With my eyes still closed I told myself, "I deserve to be on the cold planet of Venus for eons and eons. My head should be bolted down. I should be so big I fill up the whole side of the planet." I laid the back of my head on the bark of the tree. I pushed it back and back until it hurt, but that wasn't good enough.

My voices said, *"There would be a dildo in you too, bitch. For eons and eons pulsing an orgasm out of you. You would have the humiliating vibrating orgasm like you felt in the subway, even now, and you'd be dirty, always a dirty whore".*

I was cold and shivering all over. I was evil and ugly on the inside.

Just when I accepted what was going to happen to me, a sweet-sounding woman came and asked me if I was okay. I kept my eyes clinched and didn't answer; she asked again, and it seemed like the last time.

"Are you okay?" the angel asked. She looked like Oprah Winfrey.

I surrendered.

My orgasm stopped immediately when I opened my eyes and saw the policewoman. She looked at me out of concern. Her eyes were so nonjudgmental.

I looked at her relieved.

"I need help," was my plea.

Once at her patrol car, she asked me my name. The system said I was reported as a missing person when she looked me up on the computer. She asked if my mom's name was Connie Johnson.

"Mom did it," I sighed. The authorities held me in a New Jersey mental hospital while I waited for my mom to rescue me again.

When I first saw my mom again, she wore a fitted leather jacket with diamond studded wings on the back. She joked about being my angel express.

My mom flew to New Jersey and got me out of the hospital. We went back to San Antonio spending $4,000 on last-minute flights and hotel rooms.

Chapter 39

Back home in San Antonio, I went to the hospital again. My mom found a group home to put me in. She bought me a divider to separate me from my roommate. She paid for my cable so I could have something to do for the rest of my life: lay in bed and watch TV. The house curfew was 6 p.m. There were men and women in that house totaling ten residents. The refrigerator was always chained shut with a lock on it. I wasn't eating anyway. On my second day there, the lady was two hours late to bring us lunch. I put on my new dress, combat boots and carried my purse and computer strapping it in the bag around my shoulder.

I was gone. I left. I walked about five or six miles to my friend's house, but he was at a dart tournament with his wife. It was nighttime. My foot swelled up in my combat boot, so I took off the boot and proceeded on my journey to who knows where. On the way, I found a Goodwill and stole some combat boots because I had no money and was getting a big blister underneath my foot.

A few miles down the road, I trudged along in a neighborhood. I saw a house with all the lights off. I thought it was abandoned so I tried to open the door. It was around 10 o'clock at night. The doors were locked. I was tired by then, so I sat on a curb of the house. I was just resting when a police car came up.

They got out. Same drill. Why were they called? I wasn't doing anything wrong. They said I was trespassing.

"I'm just sitting on the curb!" I said confused.

"The owners called us saying you're trespassing. The curb is still their property," one of the police officers said.

I refused to get off the curb. One of the police officers yanked me up and I resisted. He put my cheek on the hood of the patrol car above the running engine. The other searched my purse for my ID. He ran it. It was nice for someone to know I was crazy right off the bat and not on drugs. Thanks to my mom for putting me in the system, otherwise I'd go to jail for sitting on a curb. I wasn't done though.

One of them handcuffed me and called a transport truck to pick me up. This truck was the kind they used for criminals. What threatened them so much about me? I wondered. I didn't get it.

The truck arrived and the handcuffs were taken off and they put me in chains in the vehicle. I asked the driver, who wasn't one of the mean officers, to put the radio station on the rock channel 99.5 KISS.

"Sure thing," he said. The driver was cool.

Billy Idol's song *Rebel Yell* was on, and I sang loud and clear for the cops outside the truck to hear me sing the lyrics.

I can see how people can die in these transport vehicles. Even strapped in, my chain gave four feet of slack. I was bouncing all over the place when they took off.

Once at the hospital, the cops put me on a gurney, my hands cuffed on both sides of the rail.

Out of nowhere, my voices told me to yell "I am the master!" from my gut, so I did. Immediately these assholes took off my handcuffs and started pushing me around. I was in handcuffs damn it to begin with! How can I possibly hurt them? I never met a cop who didn't have an ego problem. They kept pushing me around.

"What are you so afraid of? Why are you afraid of a little girl?" I kept fighting them with words.

One of them pushed me against the wall and I started grabbing his balls intending to squeeze his pigs out of the blanket.

"We got a grabber," one of the policemen said. The other policeman went to check if anyone was watching I assumed, as he whipped around the corner.

The policeman kept shifting avoiding the grab, but then he drew closer to where he liked it. It was disgusting. There was a clear difference between shifting for safety and positioning himself for pleasure.

The other policeman came back around the corner. The cop that I was entangled with tried to stop the whole struggle by twisting my head back as far as it could go, as if to snap it off. I felt in my heart that if I hadn't stopped resisting, he would have killed me.

"She's strong," one cop said.

"OK we are ready," he said.

A nurse came out to put me on a gurney again. The nurse put all of these sticky probes over my chest. She said it was an EKG.

"Hmm according to this you have no heartbeat. I just used this machine before you and it was fine," she muttered to herself. She tried three times and each time it said, "Inconclusive". She put an IV in my arm; Why didn't the nurses step in when the cops pushed me around and almost twisted my head off like a bottle cap? I wondered. I fell asleep and was in the psych unit before I woke up.

Chapter 40

When I woke up, all I could see at first were the florescent lights above. I realized I was in a hospital.

I was in the last room down the hall, secluded from the rest. There was an extra bed, but I didn't have a roommate. Thank God! I couldn't talk to anyone else right now anyway. My mom was called like she was on speed dial to the mental hospitals I frequented. She brought clothes and underwear like always. The nurses put them in a paper bag.

I threw my belongings into the nightstand drawers beside me. An employee spoke telepathically to me and drew answers out of me. Her soul whispered, "How do you feel about Bobo?" From the dead center of my chest without warning or effort on my part, I loudly affirmed that only she and I could hear, "I HATE HIM!". From the moment I entered this place, it felt like I had a swirling black hole at the center of my chest demolishing whatever was left of me.

I couldn't talk. I didn't hate Bobo! Why was that pulled out of me? The doctor came in to talk to me. I hated his smile and so I threw my warm decaf coffee in his face. The coffee was never hot in these hospitals, not for patients anyway. The nurses restrained me; then the doctor stuck me with that God damn needle full of something that left me seemingly dopey for I don't know; I lost the time and dates. I hated everyone and everything; I hated this doctor; I hated the sun poking through the blinds; I hated the sterilized smell of this place, and I hated this blanket that probably hadn't been washed since the last patient left. I could smell her dank unscented shampoo the nurses give you on it.

I'd been on virtually every antipsychotic you can think of, so they tried a new one on me.

Bobo called me on the wall phone that looked like an old-fashioned pay phone.

"Hey, Donkis, how are you doing? I just want you to know I'm always here for you," he said using my nickname to make me feel special.

I was quiet.

"You there, Donkis?"

I muttered, "Uh huh."

I couldn't talk. I was catatonic, the doctor told my mom.

"Do you want me to bring you my Ren and Stimpy slippers to wear?" he asked, trying to cheer me up.

"Nah uh."

"Do want me to bring you some of my socks?" Bobo asked.

"No," I said sadly. I turned down his offer even though I liked feeling safe in his oversized men's socks.

"Do you want me to sing you some Jimmy?" He meant Jimmy Hendrix.

I didn't feel worthy of that either, so I said, "Nah uh", again.

"Well, I love you, do you know that?" he asked.

"Thank you," I said weakly, unable to say it back.

"Ha, 'thank you,'" he repeated to me. "Talk to you later, Donkis."

He knew! He knew I hated him. I had no reason. I hated life. That night, surges of horrific images of children, I can't even say the rest invaded my mind. These thoughts weren't mine. It seemed this hospital was making me worse not better. I begged for a sleeping pill to no avail.

Once the antipsychotic got into my system, I began throwing up, my eyes flipped back, and my tongue swelled. I didn't realize it was a side effect, so I allowed it to happen as I crawled on the floor in my room with my head tilted back like a disgusting night creature staring at the lights. The effects would come and go, so the doctor never knew because I never told him my symptoms. I just thought it was part of Hell.

Throughout the next week, I had the ability to talk again. The nurses checked on me every ten minutes. It was the most annoying thing. I'd be taking a shower and had to leave the door to the shower open as well as the door to my room open. One nurse saw me naked. "Why don't you guys check on anyone else!" I screamed out of impatience.

"You are at risk," the nurse said and left. Of what? I thought. There is no way to kill yourself inside of here except to not drink water! That's it! I won't drink water!

Day after day, I laid in bed. Day after day, I planned how I would kill myself outside of here. The desperation was intense. I'd pretend to go hunting with Bobo and kill myself with his rifle, I thought.

*"You would devastate him with his own gun! He would blame himself! How selfish," m*y voices chimed in.

They made sense. I didn't want to hurt Bobo anymore; I never wanted to, but I couldn't control it sometimes. He was all I had!

My mom visited every day. "Mom, I don't love anyone, not even you," I said, and it was hard to say. "I want to love. Actually, I'm not even there yet. I want, to want, to love."

"Sweetie, it's part of your condition. Schizophrenia is like that. It's not your fault," she said. Did she read up on this I wondered? It made me feel a little better.

My uncle visited me some days.

Every day after lunch, I'd bring the root beer from lunch to my room as I collected bottles. I did not like root beer, but the bottles reminded me of Bobo; it was his favorite drink. It was, to me, comforting, like hugging a teddy bear. Having a part of someone who at least loved me and who I wanted to love back.

As I laid in bed, I felt scrolls of graffiti being written on my vagina by invisible people wanting to tag me as theirs; these entities kept circling my spot making me feel used by many.

Sometime between all this, my friend, Shawn, visited me.

"You know what I think about GOD?" I chimed.

He was used to me being philosophical. We talked many times about God especially when I was manic.

He smiled at me and tilted his head.

"Well, first of all, my sister, Darcy, said that you have to go through Jesus Christ for God to hear your prayers! That was like Jesus being a bouncer at a popular Los Angeles nightclub with the right words, style, and looks you would be let in to see the God Father," I said.

Shawn laughed.

"Well, for the first time in my life, I've been praying to Jesus not just God, but I'm still in Hell! How long does it take to download?"

Chapter 41

In the hospital, there were naked people that no nurse cared to address. There were also patients playing puzzles, watching TV or in their beds. Also, there was one lady moaning from orgasms in her sleep.

After my first week, "They are looking to let you leave soon Lara!" the nice nurse said. "Just stay good, and don't say you're a demon anymore. Why don't you try to spend more time in a group or socializing?" she said. She must be delusional, I thought. I can't be around people. I hate people!

I barely ate anything the whole time I was there. On the eighth day, my Quesada reeked of sulfur. I tried to eat it because I needed to gain some weight and couldn't. By the first touch of my tongue, it tasted like roadkill. The smell was too much to bear. I thought it was the Devil punishing me. I gagged and spat it out. I took the root beer to my room without swallowing or even being able to chew any of the food.

I tried to read the Bible Bobo bought me, but the words switched on me. It read, "Adultery is sticky sweet." What the fuck! The Devil is out to get me, I was certain. In fact, all the words changed to Satanic garble. But for others I dared to let read my Bible they couldn't see what I read. It was the Devil; he was sending me messages that I was now in his domain.

For the first time in my life, I wanted God and a way out. I had nurses read the passages of my Bible too and the words switched back to God for them. Then they'd leave and it was back to Satan for me. The whole Book was the Devil. All of it! I tried daily to find God, but He didn't care. He never showed up even with all my desperate prayers. "OK, I got faith of a mustard seed, can't you hear me calling you, God?" I'd scream. "Where are you?" My friend once said that Hell was the absence of God. This was Hell.

The Devil was all around me, but not inside my heart. I've been praying for God to save me which was pointless. He wasn't there. The only glimmer of Jesus I got was an image of him in the toilet made up of my bloody looking puke.

"If you accept me, I'll take the pain away," the Demon said. I never accepted him, but for a second, he gave me a taste of freedom. The angst inside me left and I saw beyond myself. Then I said, "Fuck you, Devil! I will never accept you!" The pain came back in an instant when I confronted him.

Every day I asked for the preacher who visited the hospitals to visit me. When he did come, I showed him my Bible.

"Look! The words are Satanic!" I said wanting to be exorcized.

He flipped the chair around and sat on it backwards.

"No. These are the words of the Bible," he said.

I rose up from the bed and grabbed the Bible.

I ripped several pages out and I could hear the Devil laugh.

"God designed you Lara..." the preacher started to say.

"You want to know who wrote the Bible? I asked.

I did not give him a chance to answer.

"God! God was manic when He wrote the Bible and we are in his simulation, a play. How else would you explain the grandiose ideas in the Bible? You all say I was manic. He was manic too! And he is having a hell of a good time watching us. So yes, I know I am designed by God!" I cursed. "Now you may go."

Chapter 42

There was a note taker that came in every day. My mind raced as she typed as fast as my thoughts rambled in my head. It seemed she was jotting a lot down. Her fingers never stopped typing but all I verbally told her was that I felt I was the Devil.

I feared her reading my mind and typing down everything I thought. I asked to look at her notes, otherwise I was sure I'd be institutionalized for quite a while. Was I seeing things or hearing things? All she typed was that I thought I was the Devil. How could she be typing so long just to write that one sentence? I asked her if she thought I was the Devil. She said if I was, she wouldn't be talking to me.

My thoughts were about killing myself and how I was going to do it once out of the hospital. Rabid thoughts about how much I loathed myself invaded every cell in my body. There were too many thoughts for me to keep up with. That's why I had to be careful with what I was telling the note taker.

I laid in bed. I was even stoic in New Jersey when I was about to kill myself. No more tears. I taught myself not to cry. I was just a cold ass bitch carrying my load of my narcissism.

Suddenly, the voice of Corey Taylor from the band Stone Sour seeped through the veins of the walls, it seemed he chose the song *Through Glass*, for me to hear at that moment. No one else was playing it. It was Corey Taylor, and it was my audible - and to medical standards - hallucination. I knew what I heard, and it was real. I rocked back and forth, hugging my legs with my head in between them, sobbing.

Then, and only then, did I show my vulnerability and a nurse hugged me outside the room when it was time for meds. I then knew for certain they had secret cameras in the rooms. Dr. Robinson came to visit me. "We are looking to discharge you soon, Lara. How do you feel?" I was so happy to be discharged soon. I could kill myself!

"Do you think I'm a demon?" I asked. He shook his head and wrote something in his notes. "Damn it! I couldn't help it!" I felt like shit.

During my third week, I laid in bed. To keep me company, I created a cloud above my head and made a visual movie of Shrek and Donkey from the movie *Shrek*. This was one of my manic supernatural talents. I didn't need TV. Donkey kept bouncing off of Shrek, trying to get him to laugh; it reminded me of Bobo and me. He always said I reminded him of Donkey.

Bobo was home from the rig. I did not call him to ask him to visit me because I was scared for him to see me like that. Regardless, the nurses said some man brought me some things. I looked and they were gifts from Bobo. He bought me a giant stuffed animal like the one that he promised me when we were at the carnival and men's socks. I felt loved. Everything was cold and no number of blankets could warm me up. They stopped giving me hospital blankets at three saying other patients need them.

My mom came every day to visit me. She always had tired, sad eyes. She came straight from work in her professional work clothes. She held together a smile, which made me smile back. I noticed she wore the diamond heart necklace I bought her several years ago for Mother's Day. She wore it every day she visited me. I was happy to see her wear it. I knew it was her support for me.

She never had anything to say except, "You're a child of God, even the Devil can't harm you." I didn't love, but I needed love so badly. I was in Hell! This was my lowest low.

My uncle was at the hospital that day. The case worker came and gave me options on where to live. She offered group homes.

I noticed lots of families gave up on their children and some patients never got visitors. It seemed the patients gave up too, on their lives.

I scolded the social worker, "You mean where you have a curfew, and they lock the refrigerator, and you bunk with six to seven people paying the same price as a studio apartment?

"No thank you. Been there, done that, but not for long till I ran away," I said.

The case worker left and gave way for the doctor to come in.

"I still don't think you're ready to leave," he said.

"Why?" my uncle asked.

"She's the most bipolar person I've ever seen! We tried to get you into the governmental hospital, but they have no beds. So, we are going to have to discharge you anyway. We need the room."

My mom was worried because I was always released before I was ready. She said I *acted* my way out. There was no acting. I couldn't; I was in Hell. You could see it had worn me down to a skeleton.

There was a patient then who stared straight into my eyes and saw the pathetic in me and I felt exposed. I couldn't hide.

My uncle agreed to let me stay in the apartment at the back of his house.

Chapter 43

"You need therapy," my uncle said on the car ride to his house.

"I hate therapy! How can I get therapy when no one believes what I see? I remember this one therapist whom I told I didn't know what was real," I started my story.

"She replied happy and lighthearted saying, 'it was okay, 'and' what was real anyway?" I told her about the time I was leaving Hard Rock Café and saw a cloud that covered most of the sky and looked like a HUGE guitar.

"She said I could make a cloud look like anything I wanted.

"I told her, no! This was real. It looked like an intricate ice sculpture. You could see in detail the strings and frets.

"She asked if I was manic. And then when I told her I was, she said 'it wasn't real'.

"But the thing is, she just asked 'what was real' like it's all subjective and then she turns around and said it wasn't real, that it was a hallucination," I complained. "That's why I don't trust shrinks."

"How come you can see it and no one else can?" my uncle questioned.

"That's a question for Divine," I said ambiguously.

The rest of the car ride was spent in silence.

Chapter 44

Once at my uncle's, I was still manic and emotionally tormented.

I had nightmares that people were raping me. Also, I fucking wanted to dismember my head from the unforgiving, relentless images my voices showed me of children! Kids terrified me after that. The first night I spent at my uncle's, he wanted me to watch a kids' show with his younger daughter. I swore in the hospital, up and down that if the voices continued to show me these horrific images, I would find a gun somewhere and blow my **fucking** head off. Sure enough, two minutes into the programs, my voices started showing me the awful images.

I told my uncle I had to go.

"What? You can't handle this?" he scoffed.

"I just came out of the hospital, and I still don't feel right, Uncle! If you only knew. I gotta go into the apartment now. I am having anxiety," I said.

"I don't believe in mental illness," my uncle said.

"Well, that is the most ignorant, uneducated thing I ever heard you say," I turned around and walked away.

Imagine my brain as a computer and the virus protection was never updated; and all I saw were these repulsive visual invasions over and over like being hypnotized. It made me scared of kids. I never told my uncle, but why was he so brash when I had just been released from the hospital?

My only real option was to go to bed and be alone for another sleepless night in the apartment. If I tried to fight these voices harder, they got louder and demanded more attention.

When I moved in, my uncle told me I could still smoke outside the property but in the woods around where a mountain lion had been spotted. I couldn't even bring the unsmoked pack anywhere around the house; I had to keep the pack in the woods across the street.

One day, Bobo came to visit me. He brought his guitar and tried to teach me how to play. He gave me a pack of cigarettes after kissing me on the forehead. "You're going to be okay, Donkis," he said. He glowed and looked like an angel. He showed me his new tattoo. It was angel wings on his back like my mom's jacket! "For you," he said and left it at that.

Instead of going across the street to stash my cigarettes, I hid them in the bushes by the side of my uncle's house. My uncle came up with so many ridiculous rules.

Hours later, my uncle came home and saw me digging through the bushes for the pack. He scolded me and threw the new pack away. I was 33-years-old. I didn't test him because at this point, I had nowhere else to go but a group home.

One day, my uncle told me he would *allow* me to still see Bobo.

That night, Bobo made an hour and a half trip down to see me and I spent a few nights at his house by the river. Before that, however, my uncle grilled Bobo when he showed up. Bobo was a 46-year-old man. My uncle was in his late 60's. "Bring Bobo in," he said. "I have some questions to ask him". Bobo came in and my uncle forcefully demanded, "What are your intentions with my niece?"

"We are just hanging out to see where things go," Bobo answered.

"Do you know she's worthless and can't do anything for herself? I mean seriously, she's pathetic. Why do you even like her?"

Bobo stopped the rant by saying, "Whoa, you don't have to go there!"

My uncle stepped back and just looked at him. My uncle was stupefied that someone would step up to him, especially to support me. Bobo and I left. We watched TV at Bobo's house by the river and went fishing. When I was with Bobo, I kept humming my mantra, "All is well," I couldn't help it. Nothing seemed well.

"There is no one else I'd rather be here than you," Bobo said as we watched cartoons.

I was high from marijuana and couldn't reciprocate the feelings Bobo had for me. I was more than paranoid on weed. I felt like a judgmental bitch. Everything he did and then everything I thought wasn't right. I was uncomfortable, alone, and self-conscious to the extreme. His eyes seemingly poked out at me. I moved closer to him, and he held me tight. I didn't want to leave, but I didn't want to hurt him by voicing my racing thoughts.

Bobo took me back to my uncle's after three days at the river house. Nowhere was truly home. Bobo was the closest person to whom I'd call home. He was my broken-hearted angel.

Chapter 45

One night at my uncle's, I listened to the lyrics to the band Korn. When they sang it felt like they were singing only to me, and the lyrics were familiar to what I felt inside. I was so inspired to share the music somewhere.

I put on my black hoodie and black jeans then snuck out of the back apartment of my uncle's house. I headed for the access road of the highway to walk to a bar that was maybe 15 to 20 miles away. It was close to midnight.

I didn't have my truck anymore because I had gone months and months without making payments. I was playing in this mania mess after my trip to New Jersey. I lost my truck as I abandoned it at the parking garage of the San Antonio Airport prior to my departure. It was eventually repossessed so now I used ankle express to get anywhere when I couldn't get a ride.

"Does Tool know who I am? Does Korn? Who else knows who I am? Actually, does anyone know who I am?" I asked my voices. "Maybe they know you," they answered. They talked to me as I veered unaware towards the middle of the access road.

A truck going roughly 55 miles per hour sped off the highway onto the access road and I was now in its path. The back of my head hit the sideview mirror of the pickup truck and the small bone of my left arm got severed after being slammed against the side passenger door. "Ouch," I said, shaking it off like it was a pinch someone gave me. The driver never stopped. This close call was enough to draw me out of my haze and I scurried towards the sidewalk.

Chapter 46

About another mile down the road a stranger stopped and asked me if I needed a ride. My voices said it was a Devil servant. I did not care; I just wanted a beer and to play Korn where I could on the jukebox.

"Where are you going?" he asked.

"A bar, the closest one," I replied.

"I'll take you there," he said.

We were silent during the ride.

He then swerved and parked his car at an abandoned warehouse.

"Is this it?" I questioned.

"It is," he answered.

"Okay, but there is no entrance," I said confused.

"It's in the back," he said.

I got out of the car, and he drove off. This was not the bar. There was a diner down the road that I walked to.

About sixteen men all walked out of the restaurant at the same time. It appears all of them had dark hair and electric blue eyes.

I couldn't believe what I saw when I walked in.

A painting of a woman's red breasts and black nipples adorned the white walls.

That was unique, I thought.

Further in the establishment I barely saw anyone, but I sat across from a man who had hollow, dead eyes. He was wearing a dusty, old suit. He looked to be a man from the underworld.

I asked him to buy me a cup of coffee.

"Is that all you want?" he asked if he got in trouble if I asked for more.

It never occurred to me to bring money when I left my uncle's.

Then, a gorgeous man, wearing long black hair, with an eyepatch and black wool trench coat, ordered tea to go. He seemed to listen and watch the stranger as I asked for coffee. He got his tea and left.

Two more men with eyepatches came in. It seemed they wanted me to get in more trouble thinking there is a significance in it all.

As I took a different seat with a student doing homework, I asked him for a ride home.

He said he would after he finished studying.

I also noticed two police officers oblivious to it all while munching on their midnight meal.

It was time. The student took me back to my uncle's.

Chapter 47

The next morning my uncle knocked on my door to inform me he wouldn't be home for a while.

He saw my swollen neck and asked what happened.

It didn't faze him that my neck was swollen, but he cleared his schedule and took me to a medical hospital.

Once in the hospital, they immediately put me in a room with another Devil's agent.

He took an MRI of my neck. Previously, I noticed the bone in my left arm was sticking out just beneath my skin. I never told anyone about that, and no one asked. In my foggy brain, it wasn't a big deal.

Then he collected around ten vials of blood and filled me with an agent that smelt like sulfur and made my skin jaundice.

Is this smell going to wear off, or is it going to be my permanent perfume? I thought, scared.

The Devil's associate smirked.

After that, while on the gurney, I heard Devil scrawls behind me as if a witch was scratching notes about me on rough paper.

My uncle's foot was tapping on the gurney. It made me feel like I was in a cradle. I asked him to stop. It was uncomfortable to feel like a toddler again.

"Fine. Everything pisses you off now. I took you here, okay? Now time to stop bitching," he said.

The Devil's agent came back in after being absent for about an hour.

My uncle said he could not wait any longer; the Devil's agent released us. The witch's scrawls ceased.

Chapter 48

My broken arm and swollen neck were old news the next day. No one talked about it.

A week later, my uncle was leaving to run an errand, I asked him for money for cigarettes. I'd been without my own for over a week. He was in a bad mood that day and didn't want to give me the money. Actually, he never gave me money the whole time I was there.

"Mom told me you would because I've been smoking everyone else's cigarette butts off the ground!" I exclaimed. I felt sick and tired of being polite. I was fed up with playing nice.

He got out of his convertible and threw five bucks on the ground.

"Slut!" he hissed curling his lips. "Good for no one, Lara! That's why Bobo doesn't even want you!" he spat.

I ran and ran deep through the undeveloped wooded landscape past my uncle's house. I scared the jack rabbits and deer that scurried away from me. I kept running.

I suddenly came upon a door in the middle of nowhere. Ram horns adorned the metal doorframe.

Bobo appeared out of nowhere and screamed my name.

"Lara! Lara!"

"What are you doing here?" I screamed, crying.

"I came to see you," he said with his big, brown eyes full of concern.

"Don't do this Bobo! I need to go! I need to run away! My uncle, my mom, you! No one needs to look out for me anymore! I'm tired of being a burden and reading in between the lines that you all think I'm pathetic!" I yelled.

My forearm raged and was red hot! Donny was calling again.
Bobo's arm reached out, but he wasn't even close.
I took off running towards the mysterious door.
Bobo ran behind me, but once I reached the door, a
translucent, warped, wall separated Bobo from me. The
touch of the warped barrier stung him, keeping him out.
I ran inside this place.
The invisible wall separating Bobo and I collapsed, and the
door locked behind me.
Bobo banged and pounded on the door.
"You're going manic, Lara! You're going manic! This is not
you!" He screamed from the other side.
The sounds of cornets, trumpets, baritones, and tubas
reached far and wide inside this place.
It was the original theme song of the circus: "Entrance of the
Gladiators."
I stepped inside, amazed by the vibrant colors of the red,
yellow, and blue balloons that were tied to the vendors'
poles and the same colors of the striped tents.
A Ferris wheel spun with kids, happy and laughing.
People were throwing balls through holes to win prizes like
large stuffed animals.
There was a woman with a beard.
A man asked her "Do you know you have a beard? Why?"
She replied, "You don't know the art of an animation!" She
believed her purpose of having a beard meant she took the
part in life as being a character of cartoons.
Why do people ask shit like this? I thought.

There were gigantic people, 11-foot-tall people, and little people. I guess some would describe them as *freaks*. I thought it was cool.

A clown on stilts came walking right towards me. He fell and broke one of his stilts when he stepped into a pothole beneath him.

"Why didn't you warn me a pothole was there, bitch?" the clown scolded me.

I thought he saw it. I stood speechless. It was my fault. I ran into a tent feeling guilty that I didn't tell the man about the pothole.

Chapter 49

An octagon of mirrors dropped from above, surrounding me! It prevented me from going any further. These mirrors were curved and distorted. It was a *Funhouse* in the circus tent. One mirror perverted my image as if I had an hourglass face. In another mirror I was reflected with a short stature and fat head. And in some like I was tall and skinny, as if walking on stilts.

The voices broke through in my head; they were melodic and seductive, deep, and sensual. It was the long, lost voices. The voice was like the caress of a sweet dream and like the rough edginess of a nightmare.

"You were never taught how to love, or you were born without compassion. Here is a recap of what you never felt. But oh, your family did." the voice said.

At these words, as I stared in the mirrors with all my distorted figures, I was stone cold. My heart was like a sullied tooth, rotting away with me.

The mirror switched to an image of my mom: static like a hologram, until she fleshed out into a 3D figure.

I wanted to hug her, have her tell me: "It's all alright, sweetie. You're a child of God, nothing could hurt you, not even the Devil."

Laughter from all the circusgoers roared through the octagon mirrors.

"I need another anti-psychotic now! This is not real!" I prayed to whomever would listen.

"Let's do a collage of your heartless past." The voice said.

The real image showed Mom and I driving on an overpass, and I opened the door to jump out of the car. She reached across and slammed it shut. "If you do that again you're going to the hospital!" I didn't do it again.

"She saved your life, oh, how ungrateful you are," the voice in the mirror said.

Another scene projected my mom waking up in a panic. Like most nights, I called her to pick me up at 2 a.m. I was at a bar about 40 miles away from her house. Through the mirrors, I saw her put on her eyeglasses, squinting, and hunching over the steering wheel to see. She hated driving at night; she had bad eyesight. My mom had to get up in a few hours for work, but I was stranded and didn't care. It was another time in the past when I was manic.

"You weren't there when she got to the address." The voice said.

I had taken off walking and hitchhiking to her house because I thought she'd never come.

Next, I saw my mom at the police station through those magic mirrors. She was filling out a missing person's report. She was crying and praying to God for the police to find me.

"Because of you, she's filed these reports countless times now." the voice said. *"Oh, there's more."* the voice said. *"Remember when she would leave work, even with short lunch breaks, and after long hours to visit you? Remember when you yelled at her that you didn't want her to come and see you, ever? Remember when she said she'd come anyway? Like a good mom would say, 'I'll come anyway, and every day; I love you, you're my daughter.' She was hurt by the truth of your words though,"* the voice concluded.

Something seemed to punch me in the stomach as I felt her pain and I sobbed. On the screen, it showed her sobbing when she filled out police reports numerous times when I went missing. *"You had manic episodes for 16 years. She never gave up. Many families would give up and put you in a mental ward for the rest of your life,"* the voices said.

I saw my mom wake up in a panicky gasp as the phone rang. I would call her late at night asking if she could pick me up from an unknown place. She almost lost her job.

"Can you imagine your mom working and smiling at clients when she never knew where her daughter was, if you were alive or dead, lost, raped, hungry or cold?" the voice asked.

"You didn't know this, but it was her birthday and everyone at her work gave her a surprise birthday gift and a cake, but because you were missing, she ran out of the room crying, leaving her colleagues, even doctors, behind," the voices explained.

"Stop! You can stop!" I screamed. I started heaving.

"They're all demons, Lara. Don't listen, Lara," I heard my mom say in my head.

"Since in mania you don't remember much, let me remind you," The voice said again. *"When you were in the hospital, your mom and Granny cleaned up the mess your apartment was in and even cleaned the puke! Can you imagine your granny, an 80-year-old woman, cleaning up your puke?"* The voice questioned.

Now Bobo's face appeared on the mirror.

He was wearing sweatpants and hiking boots with an Iron Maiden tee shirt. I fell to the ground at the sight of him. His eyes were in pain and his eyebrows were scalded, "Please!" he whispered. It was a reminder of how I broke up with him the first time. I would never forget that face! It would always haunt me.

"Shut up, shut up!" I screamed to the entity who projected this. Tears streamed down my face.

"I lost him, didn't I? The one person who gave me his all and I broke him!" I cried.

"Lara, we were so happy. What did I do?" Bobo's voice was sobering. "There is no life in this house without you," Bobo's voice said through the screen as a hologram showed me packing up my things.

"You want more memories?" the evil voice asked.

"No! Please, no!" I screamed.

"Here's more… Your Bobo cried every night and called you every day."

I started to get a push on my skull. A migraine ensued. My eyes started to roll back.

"As Bobo said once, 'I was always your friend, but you were never mine.' You yelled at him saying you didn't want to be his friend," The voice said.

My migraine thumped.

"I'll leave you alone, Lara. You don't have to worry about me anymore," was his answer.

"Remember that?" the voice continued.

I couldn't talk because of the banging in my head, but I barely had enough strength to tap out with my middle finger at the mirrors like a boxer does when he surrenders.

"Bobo thought you were dead before you were found in New Jersey. He repeated over and over in his mind, every sleepless night he replayed, 'She's dead, she's dead.' He had a responsibility, his job at the oil rig where he couldn't leave work and other lives were on his shoulders. Oil rigs are dangerous. He was so tired but had to hold down the ship. Everyone and everything relied on him to prevent the death of his crew," the voice said.

"Also, do you remember this? He stayed at your cousin's house in Dallas one night to make sure you were OK. That proved to your cousin how much Bobo loved you. He was so gentle with you. He got a hotel for you both. You should always remember that, ho," the voice said.

Now the funhouse mirrors, as if in spray paint, wrote on all the eight mirrors twice in red, they spelled,

S-T-O-P!

S-T-O-P!

My migraine subsided, and my eyes returned to normal.

The octagon of mirrors lifted to reveal a desert land before me.

I walked away from the circus.

"I get it! I learned. I need my family!"

Silence.

I walked miles.

I heard Bobo but didn't see him.

"Did you ever love me?" The air whispered. "Oh, you just cared for me," the illusion of Bobo said.

His voice elevated.

"Lara, would you even care if I died?! Well, I love you, Lara Lee and would fight till the death for us. Fight Lara, fight for your health. Fight for us!" Bobo's voice continued.

Then I heard my mom's voice, cracking a bit from crying.

"I never left you, Lara. I love you more than words could say. Remember, you're not the Devil. These voices in your head sometimes try to get the best of you! They're not real! I'm your mama. I will never leave you. Stay strong. You're a child of God."

I didn't have enough strength or energy to stand anymore. I crawled, completely alone, searching for water. Sand was getting in my mouth from how many times I collapsed.

I cried and choked from the sand in my throat. No one was around. I reflected on those whispers in the wind.

What was the train for? And the circus? I miss my family. They're all I've got. They're all that's important, I thought.

I mean, I hurt Bobo because of this stupid GPS tracker that Donny put in my arm! It would give me signs on where to go to meet up with Donny, my so-called love of my life. He was just wasted time. Time I could have spent with Bobo and my family, I realized.

I started to waste away. My fingernails grew thick and long by this time rummaging through the desert. I ripped the skin through the muscle where the GPS was supposed to be. And the GPS device wasn't there! I'd been tragically hurting people and dying myself, wasting time, and money when Donny and his tracking device weren't even there! It wasn't real. He never hypnotized me. I lost everything. I'm dead.

Chapter 50

I crawled. I couldn't see my legs and like a hologram I was phasing out. I saw a beautiful, massive door that was either hope or more Hell.

"Help." I clawed, without energy to scream, and scratched on the door with my fingernails.

"Help," I whispered again.

The door opened. Bobo stood there in his baseball cap, Iron Maiden tee-shirt and sweatpants with hiking boots. He held out his hand and lifted me up. He smiled brightly and had eyes of serenity and sincerity. He had giant angel wings spread out on his back. The wings were shining gold as if lit from above fading to a shadowy black and ending with crimson tips that looked like they had been dipped in blood.

"It's okay, Donkis, I got you," he said.

I was so relieved!

I sobbed.

I shuffled to my feet and saw my mom.

Tears escaped from her reddened, sad, brighter-than-normal, blue eyes.

My hair was matted and long and I could still see where I clawed out the GPS that was never there.

The conductor appeared next to me. In his hand he held the rose quartz that I left in New Jersey. The same one Donny gave me when we were dating. The conductor still did not meet my eyes. An image gleamed through the quartz of rock stars eating together and laughing like the Last Supper.

I did not take it.

My eyes shifted back and forth.

"Am I real? Is this real? Am I dead?" I asked in confusion.

"You've been dead a long time, Lara. When you were in New Jersey, you did jump in front of that subway train and died. In the train, you saw your life pass before your eyes."

"But it continued, your life continued. The sickness continued after you banged your head, Lara, and exited the train."

"It was your Hell, Lara," Bobo said.

"We did our time through the pain of losing you and we grew old and died without you. You had to go through Hell first and we were there in spirit trying to do what we could. Now we are at our destination. All of us." Bobo answered.

I was just so grateful for it all to be over.

"I treated y'all so horribly," I sobbed heaving. "Well, what did I learn?" I asked.

"Love matters, family is here for you," Bobo explained. "It's full circle. There is nothing to fear now. We got you. You learned."

"But Donny? He was my guide. He was my heartbreak, my heartbeat! He's the reason I put you through Hell with me. Oh, how I must have hurt y'all by leaving you and then killing myself jumping on the train tracks!" I bawled.

"Enough. You're home now," Bobo said.

"But, my uncle, he was so mean saying "No wonder you didn't care anymore! He made me feel horrible."

"Your uncle was going through his own Hell after his death and took it out on you. He was wrong. You can't judge him. He's here," Bobo finally said.

I saw my mom, Bill, cousin, sister, Uncle, and my friends. All had smiles except for my mom's tears.

Ground gave way. All you could see were stars across this blue universe. We walked as Bobo held my hand. What I learned was to follow my heart. They all stayed all the times I left. I will never leave again!

"I love you Bobo," I said hugging him.

With that said, as he held my hand, we jetted into the Everlast, and my family and friends followed suit.

Gleaming stars were everywhere. In my mind I heard Jonathan Davis's song *Basic Needs*. All I needed was this - this family I neglected to be a star in my own Universe and now I was amongst the stars in a Universe with all whom I loved.

Chapter 51

Half open, my eyes adjusted to the light of the fire beside me.

"Oh no, not again! This shit isn't over!" I thought, confused. As my eyes adapted to the scenery, I realized I was at my mom's house by the look of the sanitized wood floors. My hands were strapped to a hospital bed that I was in. In the other room, I heard noises and clinking glasses.

"Happy New Year, Sweetie," my mom said without looking at me. She was on her way to the bathroom.

"Hi, Mom," I replied.

"Lara!" she exclaimed and rushed towards the bed I was in.

"Did I miss something? What's going on? Why am I here? Why are you here? What is this? Am I alive?" I asked, searching for answers.

My sister Darcy heard something and rushed in, followed by Bobo, Trey, Bill, and my uncle.

"Praise Jesus!" my sister pronounced and dropped to her knees. She prayed and cried thanking Jesus for sparing my life.

"Donkis," Bobo gasped at the sight of me. Instantaneously, he unstrapped my hands and reached over to hug me.

"Wait! Don't hug her yet!" my mom (the nurse) said.

Bobo did anyway. He gave me a kiss on the cheek. His fingers traced down to my chin as he wiped my tears away.

"Donkis, it's going to be alright. I love you!" Bobo had a relieved smile on his face.

"I love you, too! So much! What I did to you…" I started to apologize.

"Under the bridge, Donkis," he assured me.

"Can someone tell me what the fuck is going on?" I asked as I came back to consciousness.

Everyone laughed.

"You tried to commit suicide and jumped in front of a train in New Jersey! You had a fractured skull and went into a coma for three months," my mom answered.

"Why were my arms strapped down?" I asked. "Let me guess, the cops?" I continued.

They all laughed, again.

"No, you were strapped down because the nurses said you were having bad dreams and flailing your arms about."

I still couldn't believe this was real! All realities were vivid.

"Do you remember what you were dreaming about?" my uncle asked.

"I must have been in two dimensions at the same time," I answered.

"Yep, she's back to normal. I knew you wouldn't be gone long, kiddo!" he said.

"So, again, what did you dream?" He inquired some more.

"It's personal," I hesitated.

My uncle seemed to analyze me saying "it's personal" as he looked off into space. The rest of my family was a mixture of shock, surprise, and elation.

I looked up at the angel winged figurine placed on the mantel beside me. The porcelain wings reminded me of Bobo's tattoo on his back in my dreams, rather, nightmare. The figurine also reminded me of the wings on the back of my mom's leather jacket during my episode. Then, I felt and looked at the blazing inferno underneath the mantel. The fire sounded like a sinister laugh.

Was this the end for me? Or a new beginning?